Navigating Liminal

"*Navigating Liminal Realms* is a profound g[uide to] transformative inner exploration. The authors emphasize that establishing safety is a prerequisite before engaging in deep inner work—a principle I see daily in my work as a physician specializing in integrative medicine. Their whole-systems approach ensures that healing comes from integration, not just the experience itself. Through lucid dreaming, drumming, and shadow work, the book demonstrates that altered states—whether through these methods or psychedelics—are tools, not the source of healing. As I've seen with my patients, where I utilize ketamine when needed as a catalyst to therapy, true transformation happens through preparation, integration, and expert guidance. A must-read for seekers and practitioners committed to responsible, ethical healing."

—GEETA ARORA, M.D., certified in internal medicine, integrative holistic medicine, and as psychedelic practitioner, founder of Precision Breakthrough Medicine (PBM)

"Rarely does a book serve as both a lucid guide and a true initiation. *Navigating Liminal Realms* is more than a manual—it is a living transmission of wisdom. Norma and Nisha Burton weave ancient traditions with modern insights, offering a structured yet deeply intuitive path through dreams, drumming, and psychedelics. This is not escapism; it is a call to mastery—an invitation to meet the shadow, reclaim innate gifts, and navigate altered states with clarity and purpose. For those ready to step beyond the known and into the fullness of their consciousness, this book is an essential companion."

—ERIC KAUFMANN, executive coach and author of *Leadership Breakdown* and *Four Virtues of a Leader*

"As a retired biotechnology chairman and CEO, I am enthusiastically recommending this extraordinary book. Norma and Nisha have put in writing thousands of years of wisdom, knowledge, and experience from many Indigenous cultures on healing, authentic power, and consciousness. We live in a precarious time when dramatic healing is necessary on a micro and macro level across the globe. It is also a critical period to stand up against the extreme abuses of power we are witnessing on a daily basis. The teachings herein bring these concepts forward in such a humble and compassionate way and also represent the highest ethical standards that I know. Norma and Nisha offer a synergistic approach to generational healing with very relevant case studies. My work with them has represented the most transformative learning process of my career by far, and I am forever grateful."

—JOHN DEE, chairman and CEO of Biotech Companies, with a degree from Stanford in bioengineering science and a master's degree from Harvard Business School

"*Navigating Liminal Realms* is a master class in psychonavigation, an art whose name I did not know before reading this compelling book. As a mother–daughter creative team, Norma J. and Nisha Burton possess a rare combination of deep ancestral lineage, unique educational paths, and decades of experience with the Dreamtime, drumming, and psychedelic-assisted shamanic journeying. With their unique and broad set of life experiences, spiritual gifts, and communicative skills, Norma and Nisha pull together strands from Eastern, Western, and Indigenous sources. The result is a clear-eyed, sober, authoritative guidebook to the beauty and mystery of the inner journey."

—JIM GILKESON, energy practitioner, healer, and author of *Three Lost Worlds: A Memoir of Life Among Mystics, Healers, and Life-Artists*

"Thank you, Norma and Nisha, for the immense gift of your book at such a pivotal time in the revival of psychedelic-assisted psychotherapy! As a psychotherapist with 40 years of experience working with traumatized adults, I find your teachings are foundational and essential in protecting the users and facilitators of plant medicines from overwhelm, fragmentation, and misuse of power. If used with the psycho-navigational tools you teach, psychedelics shall not be pushed into the underground again. Having experienced Norma's total commitment to safe healing, her deep non-dualistic compassion, and her authentic humility based on her own shadow work, I am filled with endless gratitude. I cannot recommend this treasure trove of practical exercises and horizon-expanding concepts more highly. Your lineage and your personal wisdom, humility, and yes, impeccability, are truly the 'path of the heart'—which your book brings within reach for everyone."

—BETTINA DEE, LMFT, psychotherapist, marriage and family therapist, and internal family systems (IFT) therapist

Navigating Liminal Realms

Psychonavigation Skills for Lucid Dreaming, Trance Journeys, and Altered States

Norma J. Burton
Nisha Burton

Findhorn Press
One Park Street
Rochester, Vermont 05767
www.findhornpress.com

Findhorn Press is a division of Inner Traditions International

Copyright © 2025 by Norma J. Burton & Nisha Burton

All rights reserved. No part of this book may be reproduced or utilized in any form or by any means, electronic or mechanical, including photocopying, recording, or by any information storage and retrieval system, without permission in writing from the publisher.

Disclaimer
The information in this book is given in good faith and is neither intended to diagnose any physical or mental condition nor to serve as a substitute for informed medical advice or care. Please contact your health professional for medical advice and treatment. Neither author nor publisher can be held liable by any person for any loss or damage whatsoever which may arise from the use of this book or any of the information therein.

Cataloging-in-Publication data for this title is available from the Library of Congress

ISBN 979-8-88850-165-8 (print)
ISBN 979-8-88850-166-5 (ebook)

Printed and bound in the United States by Lake Book Manufacturing, LLC

10 9 8 7 6 5 4 3 2 1

Edited by Nicky Leach
Illustration credits see page 263
Design and layout by Damian Keenan
This book was typeset in Adobe Garamond Pro, Museo Sans, and with Barlow Condensed used as display typeface.

To send correspondence to the author of this book, mail a first-class letter to the author c/o Inner Traditions • Bear & Company, One Park Street, Rochester, VT 05767, USA and we will forward the communication, or contact the authors directly at https://normaburton.com and https://nishaburton.com.

Contents

Preface 9

Introduction – Acknowledging the Lineage 15

PART 1: PSYCHONAVIGATION

1. What Is Psychonavigation? 27
2. Oneironauts, Psychonauts, and Reasons to Enter the Liminal .. 30
3. The Calling to a Perspective Shift 36
4. Polyphasic versus Monophasic Awareness 40
5. Working with the Shadow within the Psyche 47
6. The Three Key Elements: The Guide, the Map, and the Intent . 52
7. The Guide 56
8. The Map 60
9. The Intent 64
10. Creating the Map 66
11. The Journey to Completion Map 70
12. Three Modes of Entering Altered States of Consciousness 80

PART 2: DRUMMING JOURNEYS

13. Entering Trance States through Sound Induction 85
14. Your Brain on Drumming – The Science behind the Drumming-Induced Trance 89
15. Healing Effects of Drum Journeys 92
16. Four Stages of Entering a Trance or Dream 95

17.	Where We Travel in Drumming Journeys	101
18.	The Underworld	110
19.	Navigating through a Drumming Journey	115
20.	Drumming Journey Examples	123
21.	Integrating a Drumming Journey	127

PART 3: DREAMING

22.	What Is Lucid Dreaming?	133
23.	The Dreamer as Shaman	140
24.	Imbalance between the Dreamtime and Ordinary Reality	149
25.	Remembering Your Dreams	157
26.	Unlocking the Symbols and Metaphors of Your Dreams	161
27.	Tracking Training for Lucid Dreaming	167
28.	Attaining and Maintaining Lucidity	177
29.	Dealing with the Shadow in the Dream Realms	184
30.	A Powerful Lucid Dream	193
31.	Advanced Lucid Dreaming Techniques	198

PART 4: PSYCHEDELICS

32.	Lucid Dreaming and Psychedelics	207
33.	The Rhythm of a Psychedelic Journey	215
34.	Preparing for the Journey – Art-Making, Self-Screening, Threshold Guardians	218
35.	Setting Your Intent for the Psychedelic Journey	224

36.	Entering the Psychedelic Dreamtime	229
37.	Working with the Shadow in the Psychedelic Journey	239
38.	Client Case Studies	243
39.	Emerging – The Gentle Glide Back	249

Conclusion	253
Notes and Illustration Credits	263
Bibliography	265
Index	267
About the Authors	269

Preface

Interest in psychedelics is rising rapidly in many layers of society. From the legalization of psilocybin-assisted therapy in Oregon to movies like *Fantastic Fungi*, what was once taboo is now so mainstream it gets talked about over breakfast.

As individuals increasingly open their minds in various settings, near and far—from facilitators in therapeutic settings to medicine people in South America—discussions about the impact of set and setting, ethics and harm reduction, and how to safely navigate liminal spaces have never been more crucial.

Over the course of many years being in this field, we have witnessed both the vast healing potential of psychedelics as well as the dark side of the fragmentation of the psyche that can happen when the experience isn't held in a safe container. So it felt extremely important that we write this book and join the conversation at this pivotal time.

This book is not just a toolkit for teaching people how to alter their consciousness with psychoactive substance; rather, it is a holistic system to navigate the psyche with and without psychedelics. In much of the current cultural discourse, often the prerequisites for safe use of plant medicines are actually missing, and we feel that this is a major error.

The journey into the psyche has long been understood by earth-based Indigenous cultures across the globe, and a principal requirement is to first learn to navigate one's psyche before ingesting any altering substances. The heart of what we have learned from our Indigenous elders is their time-honored ways of training people to consciously and lucidly connect with their inner guidance systems. Teaching this pathway has become our lifework.

Who We Are

As a mother–daughter team, we bring complementary knowledge and expertise amassed over generations and a focus on working with the psyche to uncover the profound gifts naturally available to every person.

Norma Burton has spent her life leading people to understand how to transmute traumatic experiences and turn shadow patterns into gold. She has been guiding adept journeying into mystical states of consciousness, with and without altering substances, for over 30 years. As a respected elder healer, she is known for teaching from her unique combination of the most current somatic psychology combined with the ancient traditional wisdom paths.

NORMA SAYS

Since the 1980s, I have been involved in the early development of the transpersonal and somatic psychology movements, as well as the spiritual emergency approach to mental health. Having lived in Oregon for over 20 years, and with the state being the first to pass a law in 2019 permitting therapeutic use of psilocybin, I have been at the forefront of the revival of psychedelic-assisted therapy.

As a recognized mental health professional in the state, and having owned and directed a state-certified residential recovery and mental health center for many years, I was selected to serve on the State Advisory Committee for the newly established Oregon Psilocybin Services Division within the Department of Public Health. Serving as a member of this esteemed committee, I advised applications of the law and worked to establish guardrails as it was implemented across the state.

Because I have been one of the early pioneers in training psychedelic-assisted therapy practitioners, I co-authored and taught one of the first programs for the Synthesis Institute in Amsterdam. This curriculum, designed to educate aspiring psilocybin therapy facilitators from around the world, remains a standout model in this field globally.

Having guided many profound journeys into mystical states of consciousness without the use of substances, I have always emphasized the importance of drawing on ancient wisdom to navigate the complexities of the human mind. Much of my life's work has been dedicated to integrating modern psychological approaches with the practices of ancient wisdom traditions, and I felt a deep calling to contribute meaningful insight to the current discourse. While there is increasing discussion around wisdom lineages in this evolving movement, I have spent my entire life deeply immersed in these teachings. I see a need for more trauma-informed, detailed instruction that integrates Indigenous lineage teachings to offer clearer pathways into the psyche.

While there is much hope in this new psychedelic movement, I also became concerned as I began to notice shadows emerging, as they inevitably do in any movement. Some of these shadows included greed, breaches of trust, people being harmed, and boundary violations. Where great power exists, a great Shadow will always follow. This is why Nisha and I are committed to teaching how to navigate and work with the Shadow that arises when exploring the depths of the psyche—whether in individual experiences or within the collective systems we create.

Norma's daughter Nisha has spent the last decade mastering the profound potential of the psyche and non-ordinary states of consciousness through lucid dreaming. In addition to her natural proclivities, she has studied the works of Stephen LaBerge, Tibetan Dream Yoga, and countless other lucid dreaming experts. She weaves the information she has learned with masters into her own first-hand, advanced experience in the lucid dream realms. She is also a filmmaker and a leader in the immersive technology (VR-AI) field.

> **NISHA SAYS**

I felt called to write this book because of how profoundly lucid dreaming has impacted my life. Through my own journey, I've witnessed the incredible healing potential that comes from facing fears head-on in the dream world. Lucid dreaming allowed me to transform my nightmares into powerful moments of growth, leading to a deeper sense of empowerment in my waking life.

Growing up, I regularly went on drumming journeys with my mother, learning Shadow integration from a young age. Navigating liminal realms was as natural to me as breathing. I vividly remember meeting my first power animal at just two years old. As my mom studied with various Indigenous leaders and healers, I was right there beside her, witnessing a way of life vastly different from our Western culture—one where people regularly walked between the realms of Ordinary Reality and the Dreamtime.

By connecting with my Native American and African roots on my father's side and immersing myself in teachings from around the world on altered states of consciousness, I saw the common threads that weave through various traditions as well as the subtle differences. I was also always encouraged to make my own discoveries and follow my unique path. Taoism, with its profound teachings on nonduality, became a guiding light for me, especially when it came to confronting the fears that surfaced within my psyche and dreams.

I am blessed with a unique and profound upbringing that has shaped me into a bridge between cultures. As an adult, formally initiated into navigating altered states, I came to realize how my early experiences—shamanic drum journeys, Shadow integration, and Dreamwork—had prepared me to face the challenges of altered states with greater clarity and awareness.

Practices like lucid dreaming, drumming journeys, and Shadow work have helped me navigate the more difficult aspects of my psyche with increased confidence and understanding. I recognized that these experiences could be invaluable to others exploring their own inner landscapes. Sharing the techniques and insights I've gained through these modalities felt like a natural way to contribute to the broader conversation about the mind's potential and how to navigate liminal spaces.

What We Offer

This book provides techniques to engage with psychonavigation through the following three methods of inducing altered states:

- Dreamtime and lucid dreaming states
- Trances induced by an advanced method of shamanic drumming
- Plant medicine-induced psychedelic journeys.

Our premise is simple—that the ancient technologies of inner navigation through drumming journeys and Dreamwork are actually *the* essential precursor training for aspiring "psychonauts." That's because they provide a slower pace, which better supports organic Shadow integration and aligns with a person's unique internal rhythm. We believe that facilitators should be required to fully understand their own unique inner landscape before presuming to guide others in discovering theirs.

We advise that by taking the time to develop your relationship with your own higher self and the Sacred (what we call the "I–Thou relationship"), you will be prepared to be more sensorially aware and adept at navigating what arises when you do enter a psychedelic experience.

More importantly, you may discover that what you seek through psychedelic experiences can actually be accessed by directly connecting with the Sublime and consciously exploring the Dreamtime via lucid dreaming and drumming journeys. Participants frequently share their amazement at how much can be accomplished through these timeless psychonavigation techniques.

Everything you seek is already alive within you, waiting to be recognized and discovered. We are excited for you to embark on this journey into the cosmic Dreamtime with us and to become expert in reading the signs and signals so that you can map your inner landscape.

Introduction –
Acknowledging the Lineage

In Martin Prechtel's book, *Secrets of the Talking Jaguar*, he writes about how you walk in the jungle nearly blind and deaf, bumbling your way along. But one day you hear the piercing cry of the macaw, the bird of paradise, high in the tree canopy, and you think you hear him speaking to you, saying: "Search for the puzzle pieces of your life, my friend. Before you die you must put together the puzzle of your life."

Throughout this book, we will reference beloved teachers, shamans, family members, and scholars whom we have learned from. Whether directly, experientially, or through oral tradition or written works, they have helped us put together our own puzzle pieces, and our gratitude overflows as we write this book.

We hope that the teachings we share here will lay into place some puzzle pieces in your life and help you live with purpose and direction. We honor all the collective knowledge that has blended with our own lived experiences, through which we have come to craft this formula for navigating one's psyche with skill.

We come from a lineage of dreamers, dedicated to helping others uncover the profound healing within their inner cosmos. In this book, we blend our experiential, hard-earned wisdom to present our mesa, our medicine bag, our mystery school package. As an intergenerational team, we aim to resonate with readers of all ages and backgrounds through the insights shared in these pages.

We always begin by acknowledging our lineage. That is because honoring your lineage—both familial ancestry and the teachers from whom you have learned—is crucial from the perspective of wisdom traditions. Unfortunately, this practice has often been neglected; instead, cultural appropriation and the false claim of originating ideas independently have become all too common.

When you read books or learn from written traditions, a whole system of citing and crediting is in place that traces where the words and thoughts originated. However, many of the teachers with whom we studied across the world taught solely through oral tradition. We live in a culture that devalues oral traditions and this has led to an extractive practice, wherein the knowledge from many wisdom traditions is taken and not credited. For many Indigenous teachers, this has caused a deep wound and mistrust around sharing their knowledge. When knowledge is extracted without proper care it is malformed and distorted, and it no longer carries the sacred medicine it once did.

Honoring the contributions your teachers have made to your spiritual knowledge and growth creates a sense of continuity and respect. Beyond the mundane reasons of "giving credit where credit is due," there is a true energetic potency that is alive and travels through the lines of lineage. It is no longer one individual engaging in these practices; instead, you can feel the power and strength of all those who came before you, as well as your responsibility to all those who will come after you.

It's natural that as teachings are passed from one generation to another they grow and develop. However, there is a great power in being able to trace the information back to its source. If the knowledge you find contained within this book becomes a part of your teaching, please bring the continuity and power of these teachings into your own work by naming this lineage as part of your repertoire.

The Power of Familial Lineage

As well as in the lineages of our teachers, great power also lives within our familial lineages. Bloodlines carry with them experiences, traditions, and knowledge rooted deep within our very cells. Wisdom traditions often emphasize the importance of honoring and connecting with your ancestors. When venturing into our psyches we often find not only the good things from our lineage but also intergenerational traumas that have been passed down through the ages. Thus, the work of healing our psyche extends beyond our personal lives into the collective of our lineage.

Humanity's past is scattered with many painful memories, and culturally, some people have gone in the direction of trying to deny or squelch the negative aspects of the history of their predecessors. However, it is essential to integrate both the accomplishments as well as Shadows of one's bloodline. By honoring where you have come from and acknowledging the triumphs and mistakes of your ancestors, you become whole in yourselves and no longer hide from the parts of your ancestry you feel shame around.

The problem of appropriation is often rooted in disconnection from one's own spiritual ancestral lineage. If you trace it back far enough, regardless of ethnicity, all people have earth-based teachings in their lineage. Those of Anglo/European descent may feel cut off from the earth-based teachings of their own heritage and hungrily go toward other cultures' teachings with a consumptive attitude. We always encourage students to do the homework of tracing back their own personal ancestry as much as possible. Find the practices of the people who make up your genetic code and honor them. Look into the ways earth-based teachings have been hidden within other structures of knowledge and religion.

As a mother–daughter writing team, we are extremely grateful to have the continuity of our lineage at the core of this book and our teachings. It is a testament to how potent lineage can be when it is carried on through the generations. We have both been gifted dream journeyers from our earliest memories. The Celtic heritage that runs through our bloodline calls a dreamer a person with "the sight."

In Celtic folklore, a person with "the sight" is often regarded as someone who possesses extrasensory perception, intuitive insight, or prophetic abilities. "The sight" is the ability to see beyond the physical world and draw insights from non-Ordinary Reality (the Dreamtime). Within the Scottish language, the phrase *An Da Shealladh* translates to "the two sights" or the "second sight." This is the concept of being able to see into the spirit world as well as our everyday world.

Example of Second Sight from NISHA'S Lucid Dream

One night I was in a lucid state, suspended between partially waking up and partially being asleep. Through one eye I saw my bedroom (waking reality) and through the other eye, I was still in the Dreamtime. The waking reality eye saw the bedroom in the daylight. It looked exactly as it always did. The dreaming eye saw the bedroom in the dark, glowing with a strong blue color and much less solid. A disembodied voice came to me and told me this was a part of my life's work—to be able to see with the two sights.

It was clear that something inside was calling me to develop this ability to simultaneously see Ordinary Reality and the Dreamtime. When I had this experience, I did not know of the Scottish concept of the second sight.

This story illustrates how teachings live within us through our lineage, waiting to be discovered within our psyches, if we take the time to develop the skills of attuning ourselves to non-ordinary states of consciousness.

Anthropologist Carlos Castaneda wrote about a concept similar to the second sight in the teaching he received from his teacher Don Juan, who taught that every human has an *assemblage point* that appears as a conglomerate of luminous energy filaments. This assemblage point can move, depending on where one places one's awareness (in ordinary or non-Ordinary Reality). Most people's assemblage points live in a habitual place. This is what creates the perception of ordinary consensus reality that we find ourselves in.

According to Castaneda, the Nagual (the group of sorcerers of which Don Juan was part) were able to displace the assemblage point into different areas and thus perceive dramatically different realities and worlds. They also found that when dreaming, the assemblage point naturally shifts; thus, Naguals developed the skill of "lucid dreaming" to take advantage of higher consciousness in the space where the assemblage point had already shifted. One of the significant achievements of the

INTRODUCTION

Nagual was the ability to intentionally move the assemblage point to perceive multiple realities or "sights."

You can observe how similar teachings weave through various cultures and lineages, revealing deeper truths about human perception and experience. Many people, including us, have resonated with the teachings of Carlos Castaneda's Nagual community—this connection has developed through both reading their works and direct study. Notably, Carlos Castaneda was part of a cohort of Naguals, many of whom were women, who were his peers in these studies. In Mesoamerican Indigenous religion, the term Nagual (Nahuatl) refers to a person who is able to shape-shift into their power animal counterpart. Castaneda used the term "Nagual" to refer to a person who was able to "see" into the unknown.

NORMA'S Studies with the Women from This Lineage

In the 1980s, I was attending graduate school in Berkeley, California, when an astounding opportunity came across my path. Three amazing women appeared in Berkeley, ever so briefly, to teach a group of us. Deep friends with one another, they also were close friends with Carlos Castaneda and were in his Nagual cohort.

Florinda Donner, Taisha Abelar, and Carol Tiggs were quite a remarkable trio who authored several books about their lives together in Mexico: *Shabono, The Sorcerer's Crossing* and *The Witch's Dream*. They were almost like ephemeral spirits wafting through the wind into our urban setting and then disappearing as quickly as they appeared. However, for nine astounding months, they taught in Berkeley, and I was lucky to be accepted as one of the students to study with them. My time in their apprenticeship impacted my life like a tsunami.

They spoke to large gatherings on the UC Berkeley campus, yet when people heard what high standards they set for working with them, many lost interest. I, however, recognized the gold and went for it full on.

While Castaneda studied with Don Juan and the masculine side of the lineage, Taisha, Florinda, and Carol were taught by the female sorcerers of Don Juan's group. These Nagual women of power taught that retrieving our memories was of the utmost importance to becoming a spiritual warrior. They set us the task of developing our psychonavigation skills through what they called "recapitulation," a term they used to mean drawing back to your memory all your mind has forgotten—through this sacred pathway of re-membering, you gather your power. In requiring that their apprentices do many challenging disciplines, these Nagual women set very high standards.

One of them required that we wake up and get out of bed nightly at 3 a.m. and go sit inside a closet (or a small enclosed dark space with a flashlight and pad of paper and pen), and write down our remembrance of every person we had met the previous day. In the cityscape of busy life in Berkeley that was quite a task. But this was only the tip of the iceberg of the task of recapitulation. Their next charge to us was to remember "every person we had ever met."

This daunting task was designed to impress on us the importance of awareness (or lack of it) regarding our bodily selves and minds in Ordinary Reality. We cannot safely and wisely navigate altered spaces if our mind and life are a chaotic mess; we must first anchor in Ordinary Reality.

Tracking our energy exchanges extended not only to humans but also animals, plants, and the energies of the natural world. Energy is everything in shamanic work, they kept emphasizing.

They tasked us especially with remembering every person with whom we had ever had any kind of sexual interaction, because that is such a major exchange of energy. And furthermore, they demanded that, to cleanse our energy systems, we would be required to take a seven-year period of complete abstinence from sexual interactions.

> This made many would-be apprentices flee in the other direction, but not me. I wanted to know the power of the Nagual and the sacred container of energy that my body truly was. Learning discipline of mind and body and energy exchange is always a key component of the art of spiritual mastery.

The specific lineage you study with has power. Even when you work with a leader in the same tribe, each one will have their particular method that they are passing down to you.

I was initiated into the female lineage of both the Nagual and the Huichol, an Indigenous people of Mexico who had a major impact on my life. Whereas I studied with Guadalupe de la Cruz Rios, who carried the feminine aspect, Brant Secunda (a well-known author on the Huichol), studied with Don José Matsuwa, who carried the masculine aspect of the Huichol lineage. Receiving the female linage teachings of these two traditions provides its own particular way of holding power and working with "the Shadow." The teachings of a lineage provide a guidepost of understanding that others have walked this path before you. It is important to review the programming you received when you were growing up, as this is also a guidepost of understanding that leads you to view the world in a certain way.

NISHA'S Reflection on the Intergenerational Gift of Honoring the Dreamtime

On both sides of my family, value was placed on having a conscious awareness of the many worlds our psyche travels through, especially the Dreamtime. Unfortunately, much of Western society has often failed to honor the Dreamtime in this way. I feel honored to have had an upbringing that many people in our culture do not, where my dreamworlds were not squelched. I was lucky to have been raised with a mother who always respected the Dreamtime and non-ordinary states of consciousness. As a result of this encouraging upbringing,

I was able to excel at lucid dreaming and dreamwork because many of the internal barriers to such practices did not take root within me. We may not realize the ways in which purposefully dominant, colonizing systems culturally condition people to devalue the Dreamtime and non-Ordinary Reality. Being raised in a lineage that dismantles this colonizing conditioning is a powerful head start.

If you weren't raised this way don't feel discouraged. Anyone can do the work to break down the blockages toward naturally occurring altered states of consciousness within themselves.

Take time to reflect on your upbringing. What were the narratives surrounding your Dreamtime and imagination? Were you taught to ignore your dreams and stop daydreaming? Or were you encouraged to listen to the messages of your dreams and expand your imagination? Take some time to write down the point of view you were taught by your parents and culture regarding non-ordinary states of consciousness. Once you begin to see what worldviews shaped you regarding these realms, you can begin to dismantle any beliefs you no longer wish to have. As you dismantle these beliefs for yourself you are also shifting the narrative for the new generations to come.

NORMA'S Story of Raising a Child to Be a Skilled Dreamer

Having a child like Nisha was a dream come true for me. From the moment she was born, wide open dark eyes riveted our gaze with striking depth and clarity.

I remember a very early dream that Nisha shared when she was a mere 18 months of age. She awoke one morning and quickly moved the bed sheets and blanket back as if she were looking for something. Rather than ignoring that and just getting her up and going, I took an interest in it.

I asked, "What are you looking for, sweetie?"

She replied, "Mama where did the hole go?"

I asked, "What do you mean by the hole? There is no hole in the bed."

She replied, "I went down a dark hole, and I saw a tiger."

I was so taken aback, because here was my baby telling me very clearly that she had just experienced a shamanic journey. In her Dreamtime, she had gone down the familiar dark tunnel, as we do in the shamanic drum journey, and she had met her power animal, the tiger.

I explained to her that this was her friend, her helper, her power animal. She got it right away. She said she had been riding on his back, and he was her friend.

On the way to the daycare center, she told me that one of the other kids was being unkind to her there. I told her how Tiger could be right there with her, and she could call on his energy to be in her and protect her. We practiced growling and looking out of the eye with power and strength.

That was her first encounter with her spirit guide beings, with many more to come. I was so glad I paid attention to that early moment of her realizing she had powerful helper beings with her. That knowledge grew within her in many protective and empowering ways as her childhood unfolded.

The ancient teachings of your ancestors are here for you, in you, to guide and lead you into realizing your own unique giftedness and powers. A song Norma's teachers sang with her in the 1970s went like this: "You can't kill the spirit. It's old and strong. It goes on and on."

May you remember what lies within you, entwined in the fibers of your neuronal networks, vibrating in the fiery mitochondria of your cells, is this light of wisdom, this beacon of lucidity.

PART 1

Psychonavigation

1

What Is Psychonavigation?

Psychonavigation is not a term we typically hear in our daily conversations; however, its meaning can be easily understood when divided into the two words that comprise it:

PSYCHO (aka the psyche) – The human soul, mind, or spirit. Within psychology, the psyche is the totality of the mind, both the conscious and unconscious parts.
NAVIGATION – The process or activity of accurately ascertaining one's position and planning and following a route.

Thus, bringing these two concepts together, the act of psychonavigation is the ability to accurately understand your position within your psyche. By gaining access to the maps of your own mind you can plan a route within your inner terrain with skill.

Navigating consciousness with expertise is a quest that humans have been on for centuries. From philosophers to shamans, the desire to understand what the mind is and how to traverse its various states has been at the core of what it means to be human. Thus, the investigations into consciousness, so popular now in the burgeoning field of psychedelic studies, are nothing new to humanity.

Despite all the centuries of inquiry, the intimate cosmos of human awareness still remains elusive to modern science. Now researchers are flocking like bears to honey to do lab studies on the human brain under the influence of mind-altering substances. The brain has been called, "the most complex object in the known universe," by leading researcher Christof Koch.

Perception is not only altered by psychoactive substances. Many factors, such as social influences, beliefs, fasting, breathwork, meditation, and prolonged exertion, can alter your perception. When your perception shifts you can see the world in an entirely new way; sometimes it is subtle, and other times it is almost as if you are in a completely different reality. Altering your perception, you can notice things that you missed in your habitual ways of perceiving reality, thus leading to breakthroughs.

Carlos Castaneda's written works are well known. However, most people have read only his books about working with his Yaqui teacher Don Juan while using strong hallucinogenic substances. Throughout this book, we will reference Castaneda's book *The Art of Dreaming*, which was one of his later titles. In that book, psychedelic substances are not the focus; instead, reality is shifted through lucid dreaming practices.

Don Juan explains to Castaneda that psychedelics are not necessary to shift perception. However, when Castaneda first came to Don Juan, he was very stuck in his habitual view of reality, so Don Juan used psychedelics to shake Castaneda out of his stuck viewpoint. Not knowing this, some believe that Castaneda's work with Don Juan was all about psychedelics, but they were just the beginning of his journey into altered states of consciousness. Hallucinogens can be helpful, radically taking us out of our habitual perspective on reality, but they are not the only way to break out of mundane reality.

When altering the brain with external substances one should take precautions, because our brains are infinitely complex. The complexity of the mind is still a great mystery to scientists, yet profound studies at this interface of science and consciousness are now being published.

There was a fascinating study conducted by astrophysicist Franco Vazza and neuroscientist Alberto Feletti.[1] The two joined forces to compare the complexity of galaxies with human brain neuronal networks. They found that "The total number of neurons in the human brain falls in the same ballpark as the number of galaxies in the observable universe." The memory capacity of the brain is so large (around 2.5 petabytes) that a computer with a similar processing capacity could reproduce the entire universe at its largest scales. The microcosm of our individual brain is reflected in the macrocosm of the universe. Our mental computers are literally creating the reality we perceive in every moment.

To see things in this context is to realize that navigating our own minds can be just as complex as a space explorer traveling from galaxy to galaxy. Would you go out into the vastness of space without any understanding or preparedness of how to get from point A to point B? Probably not, and yet humans often haphazardly rush into altering their psyches with cavalier abandon. When altering the mind, we are dealing with something vastly complex—it requires a great deal of humility, awe, and skill. To become a true psychonavigator one must dedicate themselves to walking this pathway diligently.

2

Oneironauts, Psychonauts, and Reasons to Enter the Liminal

Lucid dreamers are often called *oneironauts,* which is a combination of the Greek words for dream (*oneiro*) and nautical voyager, or sailor. Oneironautics is the ability to travel within a dream with lucidity and conscious awareness. While astronauts travel into the vastly unknown landscapes of outer space, oneironauts travel into the vastly unknown landscape of inner space.

Similarly, the word *psychonaut* comes from the Ancient Greek *psychē* (soul, spirit, mind) and *naut* (sailor, navigator). Although it's come to be predominantly associated with psychedelic use it actually means navigation of the psyche through various means, such as meditation, lucid dreaming, brainwave entrainment, trance journeys, and mind-altering substances. Thus, this term can describe anyone venturing into the psyche regardless of the route that they take.

Jan Dirk Blom, a clinical psychiatrist, describes a psychonaut as someone who "seeks to investigate their mind using intentionally induced altered states of consciousness for spiritual, scientific, or research purposes."[2]

When you step onto the pathway of navigating your psyche with lucid awareness you can think of yourself as a voyager into the vast recesses of the Great Unknown within your own mind. The reasons you may enter into this exploration of your inner cosmos can be both spiritual and psychological. Philosophy is fascinated with understanding the psyche because it's at the core of understanding the human condition.

Cultures and peoples through time and history have grappled with what it means to work with the mind and spirit. Entering and altering the mind in order to better understand oneself and one's place in reality has been a constant exploration, from Tibetan Buddhists, to shamans of South America, to the Siddhars of Ancient India, all the way to people engaging in psychedelic therapy in our current age.

Stepping into the Liminal

Voyager, on the journey of psychonavigation you step up to a portal, a doorway, between Ordinary Reality and the Dreamtime. To be in a liminal space is defined as "a state or place characterized by being transitional or intermediate in some way." On the internet, there is a whole fascination with liminal spaces, and they are informally described as any location that is unsettling, uncanny, or dreamlike.

However, interest in liminal spaces is nothing new. In Tibetan Buddhism, the Bardo realms are essentially liminal spaces. According to this worldview, when a person dies and leaves their body, the soul traverses the Bardo realms and is eventually reborn. These liminal realms in which the soul travels in between realities must be carefully navigated. There are many teachings surrounding what to do in these Bardo realms. *The Tibetan Book of The Dead (Bardo Thodol)* is an ancient, detailed map used to help guide newly deceased souls through the Bardos to enlightenment or a beneficial rebirth. It reminds the soul to look beyond the illusions of the mind that can be scary and confusing.

Dream yoga is a spiritual practice rooted in Tibetan Buddhism that involves the use of dreams and lucid dreaming to work with the "Bardos of the Dreamtime" in order to prepare for the "Bardos of Death" after we have left this body behind. In Western terms, learning how to navigate the psyche while alive through lucid dreaming and drum journey trance states prepares you to successfully navigate consciousness at the time of death.

Regardless of your particular view of what happens after death, knowing how to work with liminal states of consciousness is an invaluable tool throughout life. Learning to navigate the psyche is a journey of learning how to safely venture in and out of various states of consciousness while maintaining awareness, and thereby successfully making it through the liminal spaces in between.

Psychological Benefits of Psychonavigation

Exploring the liminal realm between waking consciousness and the Dreamtime takes a suspension of disbelief that is not common in our culture. We are taught that reality is something very solid, linear, and "normal," and everything else is to be discounted as "just in your head." If the esoteric reasons for practicing psychonavigation feel inaccessible there are also many psychological benefits to focus on.

Death and dreams are more heightened cases of liminal states; however, we constantly encounter liminal moments throughout our lives. For example, when we make a geographical move, experience a health crisis or the passing of a loved one, graduate from school, or start a new job, these are all liminal moments. When you know how to work with your mind, you are better prepared to face these changes with skill and grace. It is a practical as well as mystical quest.

When you come in direct lucid contact with your subconscious there is a profound potential for self-discovery, emotional healing, and improved mental health by uncovering hidden thoughts and processing trauma. Non-ordinary states of awareness provide enhanced creativity, problem-solving, and cognitive function, while also aiding in behavioral change and mental clarity. When you can come in contact with suppressed or hidden parts of yourself and your mind, a deeper understanding of your life purpose can reveal itself. Coherently working with past wounds and traumas helps mend the mind. Skillful psychonavigation helps integrate the conscious and subconscious aspects of yourself, thus leading to a balanced, harmonious, and more fulfilled sense of self.

Spiritual Benefits of Psychonavigation: Establishing the "I–Thou"

From a spiritual lens, psychonavigation allows you to come in direct contact with something other than the mundane self, or "I." In the heightened state that comes from altering your consciousness, you find that you are not alone—there is something else there, another presence that comes to meet you.

Theologian Martin Buber is known for crafting the term the "I–Thou relationship." This "Thou," or other presence, may be experienced differently depending on your beliefs, enculturation, and subconscious ideas.

For example, if you were raised in the Christian tradition, it may feel like the presence of God, a being that is perceived as separate from you. From a Buddhist standpoint, it may feel more like the original nature of the mind, the "clear light" of pure consciousness that is not separate from you but, in fact, the basis of all perception.

Regardless of how it's experienced, it can be a truly transformative recognition to be in the presence of something other than the ordinary small mind. Having direct experiential contact with this "Thou" consciousness can be challenging to put into words. As the famous Taoist quote goes, "The Tao that can be spoken of is not the true Tao."

Just thinking about the vast potential of the psyche and altered states of consciousness can only take you so far. To fully understand what it means to have a beatific vision of union you must experience it first-hand. Perhaps this is another reason why psychedelics are so popular—they are a quick route to shake you into a first-hand unitive experience. However, the truth is that experiences like these are waiting for you at any moment and can be accessed without the ingestion of external substances.

Psychonavigation is about seeking the power within. A detriment of Western culture is the over-fixation on the external. This dominant culture teaches humans to constantly give away personal power to teachers, leaders, bosses, and authority figures. Western inculcation also encourages people to give away their power to external substances and situations that promise immediate gratification or release from suffering. On a mundane level, we give away our power when we believe that we can only find peace once we have enough money, a nice home, or the perfect partner. By always seeking the external as our source of happiness, comfort, and connection we can become codependent with the world. Our power is kept outside of us, and we are always dependent on external sources.

When you learn how to connect with your inner cosmology you will find that what you have been seeking externally was within you all along. The never-ending thirst for "that unnamable thing" that is missing will finally be quenched when you reconnect with your personal power. All great traditions teach that what you are seeking outside is actually within. As Tenzin Wangyal Rinpoche writes in *The Tibetan Yogas of Dream and Sleep*, "When we think the solution to our unhappiness can be found in the external world, our desires can only be temporarily sated."

Personal empowerment comes from knowing that you can have a direct connection with the sublime anytime, anywhere, and without the need for external mind-altering substances. A direct gnosis with higher consciousness is our inherent right as humans; we have just forgotten this truth. Whether you call it God, your higher self, the universe, your angelic guides, your power animal, or other names that resonate for you, once the I–Thou relationship is established you become more whole. This very real, felt connection moves you beyond being obsessed with searching externally for that which seemed to be missing within; the relationship is intimate and real.

Even so, there are important guidelines from Indigenous elders and spiritual psychology to insure that this inner relationship grows in a gradual and careful way. As Robert L. Moore states in *Facing the Dragon, Confronting Personal and Spiritual Grandiosity*, "Human spirituality, psycho-dynamically speaking, is the ability to connect with the numinous, magical god-energy."

The difference between a shaman and someone who is psychotic is the ability to touch the numinous God-energy and not be overtaken by grandiosity. That is why we are teaching you how to access non-ordinary consciousness first through the use of drumming journeys and the Dreamtime *before* working with plant medicines.

It's important to realize that you can alter consciousness internally through your own volition and dedication. As we are indicating, both in the trance induced by drumming journeys and in the lucid Dreamtime space, you are not alone. There are always two consciousnesses present: your "I" and a "Thou."

Plant medicines also have a consciousness; therefore, when you interact with them you are bringing in a third factor. The three parts are I, Thou, and the plant medicine consciousness. Our Huichol teachers instructed that one must always work with the first two (I–Thou) before bringing in the third consciousness. This is the path we walk and have experientially validated.

Even if you have already worked with plant medicines, it is valuable to take a step back and work on strengthening the I–Thou connection.

As Sufi poet Rumi famously said, "There are a thousand ways to kneel and kiss the ground." There is not just one right way. We are inviting you to explore this particular way of approaching and navigating your psyche. See if it resonates. This is an ancient pathway into the liminal recesses of your mind.

3

The Calling to a Perspective Shift

Most struggles are internal—struggles against self-importance, against binding habits, against the state of sleep that most of us take for waking—and the battleground is our own psyche.
—ROBERT L. SPENCER, The Craft of the Warrior

At the beginning of any great change in life, there is a Calling to move into the next chapter. This sense of having a Calling is a universal experience that can come about in many different ways. However, within the Calling, there is always a strong reason *why*—a motivating factor compelling enough to leave the familiar and step into the unknown. Otherwise, why would you leave the comforts of the known?

At the core of the Calling is the need for a shift. We seek out many things to shift temporarily. A plethora of external gratifications can bring about a temporary change, such as ingesting mind-altering substances, drinking caffeine, eating sugar, attending weekend workshops, or even moving towns. All of these activities bring about a new perspective, a new mood, a new realization. These quick shifts in perspective are mostly limited, though, and all too quickly we find ourselves falling back into our habitual ways of viewing the world—deeply ingrained "mind knots" will eventually lead to dissatisfaction, regardless of the external situations.

How Motivated Are You to Wake Up and Know Yourself?

Chances are since you are interested in a book covering this subject matter, you have already walked many pathways of transformation and are not a novice at personal reflection. If you've previously had some success in personal development yet still feel dissatisfied, you are primed to learn this next level of navigating your psyche. Have you felt a Calling deep within yourself to heal patterns that keep resurfacing time and time again?

Ironically, if someone has done a lot of work on themselves, they can sometimes have an even harder time shifting than someone who hasn't done much work at all. Sometimes, when one believes that they've already "done the work" and arrived at a higher level of consciousness than most people they no longer honestly seek improvement.

Take a moment to examine your own perceptions of reality. Are there areas where you've become rigid because you *know* "that's the way it is"? Don't feel bad if you have become entrenched in some beliefs; it is a constant life work to be humble enough to admit when thoughts have become limitations or prisons.

Belief can become a lens through which we filter all of reality. Think about it: The belief about what is "real" and what is "imagined" creates much of the boundary between ordinary and non-Ordinary Reality. You are not being asked to deconstruct beliefs all the way into oblivion; however, you must question which beliefs are causing you to give away or misuse your power.

What core beliefs are keeping you stuck? Do you believe that you are not good enough? That there is something wrong with you? That you are unlovable? That no one understands you? That you do not belong? These are all too common beliefs that people hold, consciously or unconsciously. When you carry such beliefs around, situations seem to bend themselves towards the belief and perfectly fit within it. These beliefs become the "because" of why things happen to us. We may think, "He broke up with me *because* I'm unlovable, *because* something is wrong with me," and so on.

The beliefs reinforce themselves and anchor us in a way of perceiving the world and every situation. Breaking a belief pattern requires recognizing the inception point of the belief and being willing to practice a shift in perspective; otherwise, beliefs become habits, a formation of tangled thoughts that we return to time and time again.

So, where does lasting change come from? Lasting change comes through diligence and dedication, walking a well-trodden pathway into the psyche to stop the habitual ruts of thinking. A permanent change in perspective is at the core of our teachings. We have seen time and time again that it is absolutely possible to achieve lasting shifts. To transform your thoughts is to change your life. Like a surgeon, you learn how to skillfully enter your psyche and dissolve the calcified places.

The Right Use of Imagination

On the path of learning how to navigate your psyche, you will learn how to use your imagination in new and profound ways. We often use our imaginations to our detriment without even realizing it. Worry is a way of using the imagination to concoct various negative realities and live out uncomfortable scenarios in our heads.

It is indeed a survival mechanism to play out possible scenarios to avoid danger. However, this survival mechanism can go into overdrive. We can worry ourselves sick. The mind is hijacked and turned into our own worst enemy rather than our ally.

Thus, part of this practice is also about reclaiming the runaway train of your mind and using imagination to bring your power back to you rather than letting it leak out in worry. As you will see with drumming journeys, when you give your imagination focused productive tasks to carry out it can assist you in getting to the root of your worries. When you reach a deeper understanding of what is at the core of your mental and emotional anxiety, you can do something about it rather than spinning out in negative thought spirals.

In *The Craft of the Warrior,* Spencer spends a good deal of time speaking about how the spiritual warrior must choose not to indulge in negative emotions and beliefs. This isn't about cutting off your emotions; rather, it's a Call to break the addiction and unhealthy high that indulging in untrue negative beliefs can provide. Ironically, it can feel good to think negatively. It can be a protective mechanism. For example, if we notice and obsess over everything wrong with us, we can try to stop others from seeing our perceived flaws. When we allow our perspective to be limited by beliefs our consciousness becomes constricted. Holding habitual beliefs binds our energy, and our personal power. Now is the time to recover and free up that energy to be used for accessing the sublime truth of reality.

Deconstructing solidified beliefs is part of the Calling and is comprised of wanting something different in your life and being willing to look at the belief patterns keeping you stuck. Sometimes the Calling is more like a scream than a Call, emerging from deep within your psyche. External Callings like a marriage falling apart or losing a job may occur. Alternatively, everything can feel fine on the surface, but internally you know that you are spinning in spirals and helplessly repeating the same cycles. You can become stuck in the same negative emotions, thinking the same thoughts, and repeating the same dysfunctional patterns.

When a Calling toward something different occurs, change is not only desired but also essential. In this book, the magical alchemy of being able to shift perspectives will be presented to you in a toolkit of lucid dreaming, drumming journeys, and psychoactive substances. However, just as with other tools that temporarily shift your perspective, the lasting shift will only come from the dedication to the deep inner work you take on.

As Carlos Castaneda puts it in *The Art of Dreaming*: "The difficulty is in breaking the retaining wall we all have in our minds that holds us in place. To break it, all we need is energy. Once we have energy, seeing happens to us by itself. The trick is in abandoning our fort of self-complacency and false security."

To abandon your fort of false security is to step into the unknown outside of habitual thoughts and beliefs. Now is the time to find the part of yourself that existed before the mind became conditioned by the opinions and thoughts of others. Your essential goodness is waiting for you. A shift in perspective is possible. Entering the depths of your psyche you will find truths rather than beliefs. So, we ask you once again, how motivated are you to wake up and know yourself?

4
Polyphasic versus Monophasic Awareness

At a conference about dreaming and sleep, we first encountered the concept of polyphasic versus monophasic awareness. From the words themselves, one can begin to deduce what they mean: In simple terms, *mono* is "one," and *phasic* is "phase"; monophasic awareness is, thus, the awareness of one phase (of consciousness). We live in a culture that is oriented toward monophasic awareness, and the phase of awareness that is deemed important and elevated above all else is waking reality.

In contrast, a polyphasic culture is aware of many phases of consciousness. They not only value waking reality but also altered states and the Dreamtime. These cultures are aware of the many places and realities into which the mind is constantly venturing.

In her essay *Perceptual Diversity: Is Polyphasic Consciousness Necessary for Global Survival?* T.W. Lumpkin writes the following:[3]

> Perceptual diversity allows human beings to access knowledge through a variety of perceptual processes, rather than merely through everyday waking reality. Many of these perceptual processes are trans-rational altered states of consciousness (meditation, trance, dreams, imagination).

She goes on to state:

> According to Erika Bourguignon's research in the 1970s, approximately 90 percent of cultures have institutionalized forms of altered states of consciousness, meaning that such types of consciousness are to be found in most human societies and are

"normal." Now, however, trans-rational consciousness is being devalued in many societies as it is simultaneously being replaced by the monophasic consciousness of "developed" nations.

Most cultures throughout history have codified and practiced ways of altering the mind as a part of life. Only in recent history has it become so devalued. The sacredness of the Dreamtime and non-Ordinary Reality has been put in opposition to the "progress" of industrialization and scientific thinking. If the mystical cannot be explained through rational thought and scientific experiments, it is not real, and for something to be "not real" means that it has no value in our world of deadlines, mortgages, and productivity.

Lumpkin's article postulates that the loss of perceptual diversity is intricately entwined with the loss of cultural, cognitive, and biological diversity as well. Perceptually diverse cultures can better understand whole systems because they can look at things in a variety of ways to understand how things work together. A mind that is diverse in this way is flexible and agile.

In a culture that relies on the scientific method of separating everything into sections, seeing the interdependent whole system becomes challenging. Monophasic awareness, which separates all of reality into categories, can become detrimental because it limits the mind. When the mind is constricted in this way, it struggles to think of innovative solutions. The main thesis within Lumpkin's studies is that organizations and systems need to find ways to validate perceptual diversity within their frameworks. Evolutionarily, it's becoming obvious that we will be more adaptable as a species if we can perceive beyond our current limited viewpoint.

Many of the imbalances we are seeing in relation to our climate, socioeconomic structures, and interpersonal conflicts come from being cut-off from holistic systems. When we see only one form of experience (reality) as valid, it makes us rigid and existing in opposition to an interdependent world. Modern humans have closed themselves off to the reality that we are in constant exchange with all that surrounds us.

The interdependence woven into the fabric of existence on this planet has to once again be acknowledged as we are on the precipice of a climate crisis. What we breathe out feeds the trees, and what they exude gives us oxygen. Without one another we cannot survive. Many of us helplessly watch on as the decisions humans have made to exit from the sustainable interdependent processes have large consequences on our environments and psyches. However, all is not lost; more and more people are being called to say no to detrimental individualism.

Spiritual, mystical, altered states of consciousness play an essential role in human availability for interspecies connection. When we see plants, animals, fish, birds, and fungi as allies instead of objectified things to be consumed or exterminated, we are demonstrating the vision of someone with polyphasic not monophasic consciousness.

Polyphasic Sleep

Polyphasic sleep is also something that has been lost in our culture, especially in the United States. This type of sleep cycle is one in which you rest over multiple periods of a 24-hour day rather than just one. A simple form of polyphasic sleep that has not been entirely abandoned is napping.

Taking naps during the daytime is a form of dipping into the Dreamtime at various junctures rather than just for a full nighttime slumber of 8 or 9 hours. Interestingly, polyphasic sleep is common in many animals and mammals. Just watch your cat or dog's sleep schedule to validate this fact. In warmer places in Europe, polyphasic sleep has continued in the form of siestas, especially when the midday sun makes it impossible to do anything other than rest.

A. Roger Ekrich gathered evidence from more than 500 references to theorize that before the Industrial Revolution, polyphasic sleep was dominant in Western Civilization.[4] Through his research he found that adults typically slept in two distinct phases. In medieval England, the name for these two phases was called "first sleep" (or deep sleep) and "second sleep" (or morning sleep).

These two sleep cycles were not limited to medieval England, however; he found evidence for them in cultures all around the world. In between the two sleep times, people would wake up for one hour and use this time to pray, reflect, and interpret dreams. This is an especially helpful practice for dream recall, because when you wake in the night you are more likely to remember those dreams than you are in the morning. When one engages in this practice of waking in the night for an hour, there can be a feeling of peace because of the high levels of the pituitary hormone prolactin that are released during the period of nighttime wakefulness.[5]

All of this is not to say that everyone needs to switch over to a polyphasic sleep schedule of napping and waking up in the middle of the night. However, it is fascinating to think that not that long ago many of our ancestors were engaging in a sleep schedule that wove the Dreamtime and Ordinary Reality more intimately together.

With industrialization came the quest for productivity at all costs and putting everything "in its place"; thus, sleep must be compartmentalized into a small portion of the night when productive things are less likely to happen. As the popularity of productivity influencers and "grind culture" rises, sleep is more and more devalued. The quest for needing less sleep so you can be more productive is held up as an achievement. The sublime creativity that is accessed in the Dreamtime is replaced with mundane metrics of success.

Collectively, if we valued the role of sleep and altered consciousness as our ancestors did, we would begin to tap into the powers of polyphasic awareness. Coming into contact with our dreams, remembering the messages they hold, and valuing them, we can see how Ordinary Reality and the Dreamtime are not separate—they are constantly informing and building upon one another. If all of reality is created in our minds, then why should external creation (waking reality) occupy a higher place than internal creation (the Dreamtime)?

You don't need to change your sleep schedule to enter into polyphasic awareness (although it may be fun to experiment with these practices).

All you need to do is make a commitment to tracking and valuing each phase, each reality, you step through.

There are many reasons why polyphasic seeing, or second sight, was persecuted, denied, and devalued. One reason noted in Brian Muraresku's recent book, *The Immortality Key: The Secret History of the Religion with No Name*, is that when humans are in touch with our "interbeingness" and our polyphasic consciousness, we have tremendous access to power because we no longer fear the death of the body.

If we regularly tune into our interconnection with all that is as a psycho-spiritual discipline, we realize that we are more than just our bodies; we are one with non-local consciousness. We come to understand the natural cycle of birth, life, death, and rebirth. In that realization, we can trust the process of being a part of these natural cycles. Instead of running in fear from our humble interdependence, we learn the way of living systems. Instead of grasping for control at all costs, we surrender and flow.

Thus, the natural healing processes for our minds and bodies involve a rhythm of growth and surrender, expansion and contraction. Construction, deconstruction, and reconstruction are natural to life on planet Earth. Growing through these cycles of birth, life, death, and rebirth is the initiatory pathway.

Sounds simple, yet it is amazing how so many structures of our education, economic, political, and scientific worlds do not value and live by this truth of the natural flow of open and thriving systems. Even the burgeoning psychedelic renaissance is being threatened by forces that want to control it. When working with psychedelics, we should steer clear of the egotistical, greedy Shadow of capitalism, the cult of personality and fame, and the appropriation and extraction of Indigenous lineages of wisdom. We must become individuated without falling prey to hyper-individualism.

Individuation versus Individualism

The process of individuating is essential, according to Jungian psychology. However, individuation is different from the individualism that we see running rampant in our Western culture. Individuation is the process of working through one's Shadows and different developmental stages to free oneself from the false Persona that has been constructed. When you individuate you become integrated, fully realizing your potential and achieving a sense of wholeness. It involves the development of your personality and incorporates both conscious and unconscious elements. Through individuation, you integrate the lost, missing, and cast-out parts of your psyche and become whole again.

One of the key aspects of individuation is the integration of the Persona (the outward-facing mask we present to the world) with the Shadow (the hidden or unconscious aspects of ourselves, including traits we may find undesirable or unacceptable).

Individuation also involves tapping into what Carl Jung called the "collective unconscious," which contains universal symbols, archetypes, and patterns of human experience shared across cultures. By connecting with these deeper layers of the psyche, you can gain insights, wisdom, and a sense of purpose that transcends personal limitations. Once you complete the individuation process the true self can step forward, independent yet interdependent with all of reality.

However, individualism has become a central principle of our Western culture. In contrast to individuation, individualism often manifests as everyone acting from their unintegrated Shadow parts. The individualistic society takes on the principle of "me first" and "I am right, and everyone else is wrong." It can become the exact opposite of nonduality. The world is viewed through the lens of "me versus the world" and "right versus wrong."

Being Called on this journey into the psyche is an initiation into completing the individuation process. Although most of us "grow up," many of us never fully individuate. We are still trapped by the unintegrated Shadow and the unacknowledged parts of our psyche.

Many people cling to individualism as a lifeboat that is keeping them afloat in the sea of constant change. The identity becomes fixed in unhealthy patterns of relating to others and the world. Even if you've done extensive work to heal, crack free of calcified ways of being, and become a better person, it can still feel like you aren't quite there. Sometimes we feel the farthest away when we are actually the closest. By taking an interest in navigating your psyche and committing to doing the work to face those outcast parts of yourself, you are walking the pathway of individuation.

Stepping onto the trail of "transitional consciousness" means acknowledging the many states of perception with which we interact and requires a greater attunement to the states of consciousness of others. Trapped in our own mind's endless thought loops, we miss the interplay of realities; in each moment, we are engaging with other people, animals, and plants that all have their own simultaneous experience of reality. Being aware of the many states of consciousness we are interacting with regularly helps us understand how we are constantly being altered by the world around us.

5

Working with the Shadow within the Psyche

Talking about "Shadow work" has become such a popular trend that some of the following information might not seem new to you. Unfortunately, many people reference or bring up Shadow material without actually knowing what to do with it; they nudge the Shadow without the proper tools and container to safely sequester and transmute it, which can be just as damaging as ignoring it.

However, the Journey to Completion developed by Norma is a holistic, living system that safely holds the process of drawing forth the Shadow and transmutes the Shadow pattern fully.

Shadow work in relation to psychonavigation involves learning how to see the blind spots within your psyche. Contacting how we *really* feel and what we *really* think can be an elusive task; we have defense mechanisms built up to protect ourselves from being hurt by others. These same defense mechanisms can also keep us from knowing our innermost selves.

The Shadow is actually a split in consciousness that occurs. We begin life with our essence self, the *child mind*, in a state of original goodness. But when a traumatic or troubling situation happens to us, the psyche splits: Part of us goes "above ground," so to speak, and forms our "Persona," the acceptable part of us we show the world; the other part of us goes down into the unconscious and becomes our "Shadow," or hidden-away part, and it can be threatening to admit it into our conscious awareness.

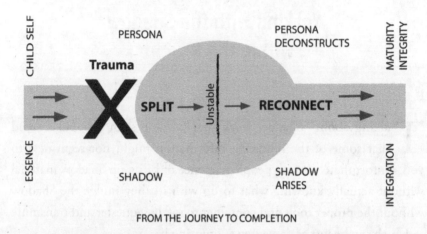

Fig. 1: Seek Safe Container

Norma created this diagram to demonstrate the formation of the Persona and Shadow in the human psyche. Every human undergoes this kind of splitting of the consciousness when trauma occurs.

NORMA'S Description of the Diagram

I developed this diagram after reading about a fascinating quantum physics experiment. The scientists wanted to observe what would happen to a coherent beam of light when it was directed at a wall that it could not go through but had to split and go around. They posed the following question: After the split occurred, would the light beam continue to travel in the two opposite directions forever, or would it come back together at some point to reform into one coherent beam?

The scientists discovered that as soon as the two split sections of the beam of light reached the end of the wall, right away the light beam reunited into one coherent light beam. Over and over this test was repeated and each time, as soon as it was possible, the split light found a way to reunite into its wholeness and coherency. This led me to a comparison between this coherent beam of light and the human psyche. When it is forced to split out of its original coherence or wholeness due to a traumatic incident, the psyche has a compelling Intentionality to try to reunite into wholeness as soon as possible. Thus, a traumatized person has an inner drive to find a safe enough container in which the split can be recognized and healed.

Often, humans look for this container in a love relationship. This can work at times, but more typically both partners in the relationship are simultaneously triggered by their Shadow issues; the couple relationship is often not safe enough to accomplish this deconstruction and integration process on its own. As a result, for millennia, people have sought out a safe container by going to the fringe of their society to find a trusted elder, a healer-shaman. Nowadays, this person can also be a therapist or psychedelic facilitator. Within that expertly held container, the psyche can begin to relax.

Establishing the safety of the container is a prerequisite for the next step, wherein the Persona must be safe enough to deconstruct over time and the Shadow defenses must be allowed to show themselves and rise into view. Then, with skilled help, the psyche can see its way through to the integration of the gifts a person's Shadow has been faithfully storing for them until the right moment.

As the great mystic poet William Blake wrote in *Songs of Innocence and Experience*, the soul travels from its original innocence into the challenges of experience and eventually returns to an innocence that is now wise and informed by integrating the gifts from the trauma wound.

The Outer Shadow and the Inner Shadow

A uniquely effective factor of the Journey to Completion system is that the Shadow is divided into two parts: the *Outer Shadow and the Inner Shadow*. No other system of working with the Shadow frames it in this exact way.

> **NORMA'S** Unique Method to Accurately Track the Shadow in Our Psyche
>
> After extensive study of how the Shadow processes work—the result of years learning Jungian psychology and developmental psychology, undergoing Huichol shamanic training, and counseling thousands of people—I devised a method of accurately tracking and sequestering our Shadow dynamics by dividing it into two parts: the Outer Shadow and Inner Shadow. This way of sequestering the Shadow does not exist in other forms of Shadow work that are currently out there, and it is a core piece of how I teach my students to deal with the Shadow.

When someone outside of you appears threatening or irritating, they are acting in the role of your **Outer Shadow**. They represent to you a pattern in your life in which you have felt oppressed or victimized. People appear in your current life playing this Outer Shadow role, then the Shadow pattern energy is replicated time and time again with different people. We trace it all the way back to its inception point, where the primal wound occurred with a key person in your life.

Our parents or early caretakers lay the template of our Shadow wound patterns, then different people appear to play out these same dynamics over and over. That is why you can go through life feeling like you are dealing with different versions of the same irritating people. For example, you may break up with one partner only to find that your next partner has the exact same triggering personality traits. This is because they are playing *your* Outer Shadow. You may even be helping others to play it so well for you.

The **Inner Shadow** refers to your feelings and behaviors in response to this triggering Outer Shadow person. You may have felt sad, surprised, confused, angry, but then acted patient, accepting, quiet, forgiving, so it is important to note both your feeling and your behaviors in response to the Shadow.

The study of the Outer and Inner Shadow is done with the help of the *Outer/Inner Shadow* chart. In The Journey to Completion, the Outer Shadow is viewed as a distorted version of your missing, disowned characteristics. At some point, these characteristics were deemed unsafe or unacceptable, traumatically dislodged, and thrust into your unconscious. Now, through the recurring irritants in your life, your Shadow reminds you of the need for integration.

Outer and Inner Shadow Chart

Outer Shadow	Inner Shadow
Name the person who irritates or oppresses you and list adjectives that describe what they do.	List adjectives describing your feelings and behaviors in response to the Outer Shadow.
- Demanding - Self-righteous - Critical - Blaming - Self-centered	- Shut Down - Go Numb - Retreat - Defend - Accommodate

Fig. 2: The Outer and the Inner Shadow

6

The Three Key Elements: The Guide, the Map, and the Intent

Within many wisdom traditions, the explorer of consciousness would take on a journey into the psyche as they would a vision quest to a far and dangerous land: following great preparation beforehand. This would include cleansing, wearing ceremonial clothing, fasting, making long pilgrimages, and carefully thinking about their Intent. After an entheogenic encounter (ingestion of a psychoactive substance to produce a non-ordinary state of consciousness for religious or spiritual purposes), they would take time to digest the results for years. It's serious business to explore the wounded places within, so the wisdom lineages approach this task with great care.

According to the Huichol, the purpose of such a journey is to seek entrance into the numinous universe through the *Nierica* (sacred portal). You do this to receive a more accurate reading of reality. By entering the portal into altered reality, you obtain information, healing, and power that you can use here on this earthly plane of existence. Bringing back the powers from the "other side," you improve your life and the lives of your community; therefore, the Huichol do not journey for recreation or distraction. Harvesting and interacting with plant medicine is approached with great respect and with balanced reciprocity.

A common mystical concept is the healer who becomes adept at traversing the axis mundi, the great sacred mountain, the tower between the worlds, to bring back knowledge from the other worlds to better the lives of their community. When you ingest plant medicines or engage in lucid dreaming and drumming journeys you are traveling along this axis mundi. The Latin term *Axis mundi* means "axis of the world," or cosmic axis. It is the point where the earthly plane meets the higher spiritual realms. In the Bible, Jacob dreams of a ladder that stretches between Heaven and Earth, and angels go up and down the ladder. The axis mundi is often depicted as a tree, ladder, mountain, or pillar.

YGGDRASILL,
The Mundane Tree

Fig. 3: Yggdrasill, the mundane tree (illustration by Finnur Magnússon, 1859)

The axis mundi is an ancient concept and has appeared independently in various cultures and religious traditions around the world. It is difficult to pinpoint a single origin, as it seems to arise naturally from human attempts to understand and symbolize the connection between the earthly and the divine.

Our own mind/body can also be viewed as an axis mundi between the worlds. Perceptually, we are the center of our reality, and from that space, we can move to make new discoveries and establish new points of contact as we enter into various realms of consciousness.

It is a profound realization that we have this ladder within us. In the ancient Indian Hindu tradition, the *kundalini* ladder goes up and down our spine, and awakened kundalini energy rises and descends along energy centers known as *chakras*. Our body/mind is a precious conduit of this connection between Ordinary Reality and the Dreamtime.

One of our shaman guides from Peru noted that he saw many people come to take part in an ayahuasca plant ceremony who were untrained in navigating the ladder up and down. Ayahuasca would take them up and then they got stuck as they did not know how to come back down. In order to travel this path, it is wise to have certain elements in place that create a safe vessel to travel within.

NORMA'S Findings on the Container Needed to Navigate the Liminal

Shocking as it may seem now, not that long ago, when I was studying at university in the 1970s, I could find only one book that gave any credence to the healing potency of ancient shamanic medicine practices. It was written by Mircea Eliade, a University of Chicago professor in the 1950s, who, having received a large grant to travel the world visiting Indigenous cultures, set out to explore what the word "shamanism" meant, resulting in his dense anthropological study, *Shamanism: Archaic Techniques of Ecstasy*.

When I found this rare gem, I read it over and over, gleaning all I could from Eliade's first-hand encounters with Indigenous shamanic cultures.

One thing that stood out for me was that Indigenous cultures specializing in healing through altered states had three things in common:

THE THREE KEY ELEMENTS: THE GUIDE, THE MAP, AND THE INTENT

They each taught that a psychonaut must find a GUIDE, a MAP, and a CLEAR INTENT.

- **A Guide**: You had to find a guide to take you on the journey. Because the journey always involves facing into one's own Shadow, to ally with a masterful guide is the best approach to ensure that you make it all the way through to the other side of the quest.
- **A Map**: The guide will show you a map of consciousness that you follow carefully on your journey. When you see a true map of consciousness, deep within your soul you will recognize it as resonant.
- **A Clear Intent**: After showing you the map, the guide will help you set your own clear Intent. The ultimate success of the journey depends upon the Intent and good-hearted, humble, sincere questing of the journeyer.

In the following chapters, we will explore each of these three elements in more depth so that as you prepare to take your journey you ensure that you have the adequate elements in place.

7

The Guide

Our teachings are for all, not just for Indians....
The white people never wanted to learn before. They thought we
were savages. Now they have a different understanding, and they
do want to learn. We are all children of God. The tradition is open
to anyone who wants to learn. But who really wants to learn?

—DON JOSÉ MATSUWA, Huichol, 1989

Don José Matsuwa and Guadalupe de la Cruz Rios were partners in teaching a group of Westerners the inner workings of how the Huichol approached integrating the Shadow. Some of us in the 1970s and 80s were lucky enough to be part of a select group of students who got to learn directly with them over many years.

Fig. 4: Guadalupe de la Cruz Rios (photo by Vita Rose, 2007)

THE GUIDE

To find an appropriate guide one must learn the skill of discernment and how to follow their intuition. Don't select a guide just because other people say they are great. You need to get a clear "hit" within yourself that this is the right person to take you along the journey. When you apprentice with a guide, you must have a deep level of trust in their guidance. Opening up your psyche to another person is not to be taken lightly. If entheogens are involved in your work with a guide, it is even more essential to trust what they are seeding into your psyche, because it is much more neuroplastic than it usually is.

Even in more casual settings, it is good to be cautious about who you let influence you when in an altered state. The term "set and setting" has become popular in the current iteration of psychedelic therapy. Having the right setting or environment to enter into non-ordinary states of consciousness can make all the difference. Even if you are just taking psychedelics recreationally, you are still opening up your spirit and psyche on a deep level. The thoughts, beliefs, and ideas of others can unconsciously take root in your psyche, whether you want them to or not. When letting someone guide you, remember it's always okay to say no if the situation no longer feels safe. Connecting to your inner guidance first and foremost is one of the most important things you can do.

NORMA'S Work with Her Guides

Throughout my younger years, I felt compelled to seek out elders who could show me the way to the alchemical transmutation work of the soul. The question was, who could guide me on an authentic pathway toward this wholeness?

Thankfully, I had a really strong bullshit meter. In my 30s, I was able to get close to many authors of great books and famous spiritual leaders. However, when I got to know them, I got to see how they were mixed-up, shadowy characters who were really misusing their power. It became pretty discouraging. When I did find authentic, integrated, healthy, kind, wise elders it was like finding nuggets of pure gold.

To name some of my profound teachers:
- Guadalupe de la Cruz Rios, my Huichol grandmother, and her niece Maria
- Tate Angela, master teacher of Orisha and Espiritu school in Brazil
- Grandma Aggie Baker Pilgrim, Takelma elder in Southern Oregon, founder of the Thirteen Grandmothers
- Taisha Abelar, Carol Tipps, Florida Donner: Yaqui Nagual with Don Juan/Carlos Castaneda
- Sobonfu and Malidoma Patrice Somé, African Congolese shaman and authors
- Goinka-ji, first brought Vipassana Buddhist meditation to the United States in the 1970s
- Thich Nhat Hahn, Zen Buddhist master
- Dr. Archie Smith, Psychology of Religion and Black Theology professor at Pacific School of Religion, Berkeley, California
- Kathy Sanchez, Tewa, New Mexican curandera, founder of Tewa Women United
- Larry Littlebird, Laguna/ Santo Domingo Pueblo, New Mexico, tribal elder, storyteller, filmmaker, author.

The metric for finding a suitable teacher boils down to their actions, not just words. I found I could deeply trust my teachers because they did not misuse their power. They were not defensive, they did not hold themselves above others, and they did their own Shadow work repeatedly. I watched them in all kinds of circumstances, and they were clear and impeccable in various challenging moments.

Having healed the Shadow of shame and blame, they were able to admit when they were wrong. Operating from a non-dualistic or non-judgmental space, I witnessed time and time again how they would humbly admit their weaknesses, forgive, and "walk their talk." I aspired to be a leader like them and worked at it for years. Because I knew I could trust them, I diligently followed their instructions. I participated in 10-day, 21-day, and 30-day silent retreats. I underwent numerous wilderness initiations and fasting ceremonies.

   Furthermore, I submitted myself to intense plant medicine journeys under their guidance. This pathway I chose to walk was not an easy one. My teachers showed me how to examine my self-importance, my projections and triggered reactions, and my own misuses of power. Malidoma Patrice Somé, an African Congo shaman (husband of Sobonfu Somé), once told us if you think you have a Calling to be a shaman healer, run the other way if you can. It's not an easy path.

We encourage you to engage deeply with this book, not just as a reader but as an active participant. Immerse yourself in the practices of trance drumming and dreamwork to navigate the intricate landscape of your psyche. Mastery comes through dedication. Spend time learning from teachers and immersing yourself in these practices before guiding others. Your ability to be a skillful guide is directly tied to how well you've explored your own inner world, resolved energy blockages, and healed any misuses of power.

   This book serves as your guide into the depths of your psyche, leading you on a well-established path to help you better understand and work with your inner self.

8

The Map

The process of map making, whether for outer terrain or inner terrain, is done the same way. One is taught experientially to walk the pathway and track and document everything one encounters along this way and learn from it. The voyager then comes to tangibly understand the terrain and can make a personal map based on this understanding. This way of teaching humans about the inner cosmos, this map-making pedagogy, is as old as time and endures.

Frequently, people experimenting with psychedelics in our current times are missing a clear map. This can sometimes result in them getting lost in the depths of their unintegrated traumas or unable to find their way back down the ladder into a grounded life in Ordinary Reality.

Guadalupe told us that as we learned to psycho-navigate following this ancient map, step by step through the maze of our unconscious, we would learn what "completion" means—that one revolution around this journey circle would correspond to healing one theme of our Shadow patterns.

Walking this ancient pathway can be compared to weaving a rug, she said. You pick up a strand of yarn, which is like taking up the Calling to study and heal a certain theme of your Shadow that is ripe, then you intricately walk the circle, which is like pulling the thread all the way through the weaving and tying it off; that one strand of the rug is then woven in and completed. Later, working on integrating the next gifts of the Shadow, you pick up another strand of yarn and gradually bring that one all the way through.

As you walk this path throughout your life, constantly weaving thread after thread of your Shadow work through to completion, you come to the end of your life, and you have woven a whole beautiful "rug." By faithfully walking this path over and over again, Guadalupe assured us, we will have brought our whole incarnational destiny path through to completion by the end of our lives. The rug is complete. That is a very hopeful evolutionary vision.

Cross-culturally, there are examples of maps that have been drawn to show the pathway into and out of the collective unconscious. Within this framework, there is the collective map and your personal map: the macrocosm and microcosm. The voyagers' job is to use the collective map to carefully venture down into their psyches and then chart the terrain of their own personal landscape, creating their own map.

The Map of Plato's Cave

When you explore maps of various cultures around the world you discover a common theme. Within Western philosophy, Plato explored concepts like the soul (*psyche*) and reason (*nous*). Plato's famous allegory of the cave can be looked at as a metaphorical mapping of human perception.

Fig. 5: Drawing of Plato's "Allegory of the Cave." (Markus Maurer)

Prisoners are chained to the wall in a cave where they can only see the cave wall. They accept the shadows on the wall as if that is the only reality and do not question if another reality could exist beyond that. This partial and distorted reality is the one most people live in, according to this allegory. People who perceive these limited sensory experiences could be compared to people only interacting with mundane reality and thinking that is the totality of the experience of consciousness. This can also be compared to the Buddhist understanding of ignorance—not knowing the full truth of our inherent enlightened nature.

One prisoner eventually breaks free and ventures outside the cave. This breaking free represents the journey of philosophers out of ignorance into knowledge. The sun is a representation of enlightenment and the highest truth that one can understand on this pathway.

It's impossible to fully explain the sun to someone who has never seen it before. You can give them a sense of what it is, but to get the full impact, they must have a direct experiential knowledge or *gnosis* of the sun. This allegory points to the fact that what we can perceive of the world from our senses is not all of reality but rather, just reflections of the totality of reality—like shadows on a cave wall. Perception is constrained by ignorance and consensus reality.

The journey out of the cave is the adventure into the numinous states of reality that can be experienced and the different levels of consciousness that exist. Once the prisoner has seen the larger scope of reality, he returns to the cave to share his findings. This emphasizes the importance of returning and faithfully communicating your experiences. In this way, you integrate the experience back into your daily community life and help your community by sharing your findings.

The Map of the Self

Different stages of consciousness have been mapped in various ways. Sigmund Freud broke down the psyche into the *id,* the *ego*, and the *superego*. The id is the impulsive pleasure-seeking and pain-averse part, the superego is the morally correct judgmental part, and the ego is the conscious part of your personality that mediates between the other two. Carl Jung, who studied with Freud, included the conscious mind, personal unconscious, and collective unconscious within his modality of understanding the psyche.

Similarly, within Hinduism, the self is broken down into Atman, which is the individual self, and Brahman, which is universal consciousness or ultimate reality. In texts like the *Mandukya Upanishad*, consciousness is further broken down into various states such as waking (*jågrat*), dreaming (*svapana*), deep sleep (*suṣupti*), and the transcendental state (*Turiya*) of pure consciousness that exists beyond and within the other three states.

Tibetan Buddhism breaks down these states of consciousness in a strikingly similar way, pointing to dreaming, deep sleep, and the pure light of consciousness that exists beyond and within all other states as well.

When we see how interrelated all of these maps of consciousness truly are, we begin to understand that there is a deeper truth that exists cross-culturally about the components of the psyche and the mapping of the pathway. As Marc Aixalà stated in the book *Psychedelic Integration*: "During the first few years, most of my interventions happened 'in the dark,' so to speak, lacking useful maps that could guide the psychotherapeutic process. In 2015, after doing this work for a few years, I began to recognize common patterns."

Recognition of the Map

As the initiate, some deep part of you will recognize a good map and its validity when you first glimpse it. You will feel an innate, heartfelt trust in the map maker, and feel Called to walk the path. Only when that trust and alignment is felt should the journey begin. Throughout time, psychonauts have dedicated themselves to making conscious the study of their psyches and understanding where their minds are residing in any given moment. Becoming a psychonaut is more than just learning about how to travel into psychedelic experiences with skill; it is about building skills with consciousness so that you can live with more presence.

9

The Intent

As Carlos Castaneda famously wrote, "Intent is everything." The power to clearly identify your Intent when going into the unknown cannot be overstated. Think of your Intent as what leads you to the treasure chest at the end of a pirate's map. It is the reason for the hero to go on her quest, the propelling force that enlivens you even when the situation is dire.

On this quest into your psyche, you are tracking and stalking your personal power—what you must have next in your life. As in any great journey, there will be obstacles, challenges, and monsters to face. Intent is what keeps you moving.

Within great stories, the protagonist has a clear Calling that propels them forward. This Calling is so strong that they can no longer continue on with life as it was; they must make an internal shift. If they do not make this shift, then the story is a tragedy rather than a heroic journey. The reason this story structure resonates so deeply with humans is because it is an ancient truth of human life. We all have places where we begin to get stuck and eventually, those ruts become so unbearable that to not take on an internal journey of growth would be a tragedy.

While we may generally think of these as external journeys, such as in stories like Odysseus voyaging across the seas to Ithaca, every outward quest is also combined with an internal journey of growth. As you venture into your psyche, you are embarking on an internal journey. Beautiful treasures are waiting for you, and your Intent *can* be accomplished.

Before gaining the gifts waiting at the end of the quest, we must first remove ourselves from the role of victim. It is a radical act to take responsibility for our perception of reality. The power of perception is oftentimes diminished; however, perception is how we shape the reality around us. We hold beliefs, conscious or subconscious, that form our entire ways of perceiving reality, yet most of the time leave them unexamined and unquestioned.

As you move into taking self-responsibility you will notice the areas in your life where you have been holding onto outdated beliefs that are harming you. Tracking the threads of those beliefs to their inception point is the work of the psychonaut, and the map we have laid out is the way to do that.

By clarifying your Intent, you are dedicating yourself to working through beliefs, thought patterns, and habitual actions that are discordant with the Intent you hold for your life. An unbending Intent helps you synchronize your mind, body, and spirit toward actualizing your Intentions. This is a key aspect of impeccability—you formulate a plan and follow it.

Before entering the initiation in the Dreamtime, many Wisdom Traditions put participants through a screening and preparation process. In the Journey to Completion system, there is a naturally embedded screening process at the Threshold. We pause at the Threshold because it is an important moment to test ourselves before crossing into non-Ordinary Reality, to see if we are truly ready for the journey we are about to embark on. Having a strong and clear Intent will be what carries you through your entire journey. That is why it is of utmost importance.

10

Creating the Map

We will now share with you the Journey to Completion Map. Although this text is not dedicated to teaching you the full process of the Journey to Completion, it is embedded within all our teachings as the core principles. A good guide will always present the student with a complete map to view.

If you encounter a guide or teacher who is withholding the full process, or only offering to take you into the Shadow realms (the deep unconscious, the Underworld) without showing you a clear way back out, this is not someone you should trust with your psyche. The trustworthy guide will always begin by sharing the overview of the complete map and assuring you that if they are taking you in, there is a way to get through and back out, more whole and complete.

Mircea Eliade once stated that a shamanic guide who is a true healer begins by sharing "the map of consciousness." Some deep part of the student recognizes it as valid, trusts the map maker, and feels Called to walk this path. Then the journey begins. By glimpsing and understanding this fuller system of the Journey to Completion Map you will be able to recognize the steps being presented throughout this book and orient yourself around them.

> **NORMA'S** creation of the Journey to Completion Map
>
> I created this map in 1995, on the heels of my long apprenticeship with the Huichol people. And now I have been teaching students how to walk this pathway for nearly 30 years. Also reflected in the teachings of this map is my career as director of battered women's shelters, being on the frontlines of dealing with complex trauma at the very core of our culture, and the misuse of power over others.

The map also draws on the best of my extensive graduate-level academic training in counseling psychology and the psychology of religious experience. During those years of grad school in the San Francisco Bay Area of California, I was one of those privileged to work closely with Stan Grof and the Spiritual Emergency Network of therapists. I was at the forefront of the transpersonal psychology movement, as we went about proving the effectiveness of spiritual technologies for treating extreme psychological states, even psychosis and DID (Dissociative Identity Disorder).

During those days I had an unexpected encounter with an old shaman woman right in the middle of the UC Berkeley campus. I will never forget the day I first met Grandmother Guadalupe, the Huichol marakame (master healer) who would become one of the most important spiritual guides in my life. She had been helped to come from Mexico for a brief visit to Berkeley to try to raise money for her tribe, who were being displaced from their lands by the invasion of a mining company. When I spoke with her after their presentation, she looked me right in the eye and promised, "You can come to completion." That promise sparked my curiosity.

So I spent as much time as possible with her over the next 20 years. Eventually, after what was to be my final, extremely intense, 13-day peyote ceremony with her, she told me that my medicine bag was complete and I had permission to teach the pathway she had gifted me. Shortly after that time together, she passed away.

I took her commission utterly seriously and set out to try to arrive at my own way of communicating this incredible pathway to others. What I came up with was a map. It took two years of mulling over and remembering all my experiential moments with her to find a way to summarize it adequately in a map, or codex diagram.

The map of this Journey to Completion holds the intricate details of how to sojourn into the deep unconscious, retrieve your own lost parts, and then be able to accurately embody the energetic gift of the Shadow, and integrate its powers into your daily life in order to forge a new identity successfully.

After Doña Guadalupe gave me permission to pass along the teachings, I took on the task of being a bridge person. Teachings from other cultures can be hard to understand from our Western viewpoint and often get misinterpreted or misunderstood, so I took great care when bringing the oral teachings into a written form. I drew from not only the teachings of the Huichol but also all of my comparative religions and psychology studies to build this complete system of entering and exiting the Dreamtime in order to receive its gifts.

About five years after creating the map, I read Joseph Campbell's book *The Hero's Journey*. Campbell had traveled all over the world researching Indigenous cultures and had found this pattern of transformation that humans seemed to follow. I hadn't seen Campbell's map before creating my own; however, when I laid eyes on his *Hero's Journey* map, my heart leaped. It was very similar to the map I had created simply by trying to describe my own lived experience in the journey work with the Huichol.

This was a tremendous affirmation that what I had experienced and transcribed was a piece of Truth. If you notice similarities between the *Hero's Journey* and this map, it is because there is a real and authentic teaching system and pathway that has existed in a similar form since ancient times all over the planet.

The Journey to Completion Map is a living system, imbued with a power that you feel when you enter into it, just like you feel when you take a plant medicine. This map gives you an overview of a landscape you will be getting to know much more intimately. You walk the pathway well trodden by countless human voyagers from the time before time, in the days of the religion with no name.

As a living system, you engage with it. You are being met and interacted with. You are not alone in a living system. The map shows you the way that some deep part of you has always known into direct contact with an energy system that sustains this planet.

In the next chapter, we will show you the map of the Journey to Completion, which teaches you how to enter into the psyche in a careful way and exit, having retrieved profound gifts.

11

The Journey to Completion Map

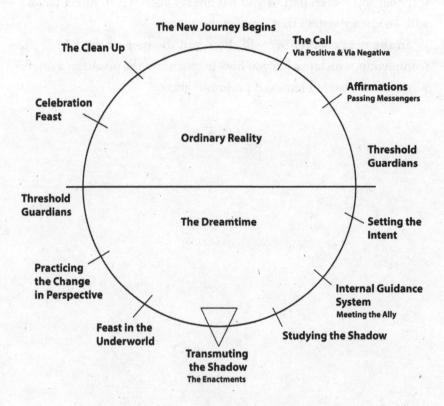

Fig. 6: The Journey to Completion Map (Norma Burton, 1997)

When looking at the Journey to Completion Map, note that it is divided into two sections: Ordinary Reality and The Dreamtime. The journeyer travels around the circle in a clockwise direction, beginning with "the Call," then continuing down into the Dreamtime, the Underworld. This act of crossing over from Ordinary Reality into the Dreamtime is at the heart of all altered-state experiences. Becoming skilled at psychonavigation involves knowing how to expertly move between the two states of consciousness.

In this framework, the Dreamtime is not limited to the state you experience when asleep; it also encompasses meditative states, trance states, and psychedelic states. In many traditions, it is also viewed as the Underworld, the unconscious, and the realms of the dead. In upcoming chapters, you will learn how the Underworld does not have the same negative connotations it does in some interpretations of Christianity. For the purpose of this discussion on psychonavigation, think of this word as referring to your own deep unconscious.

Let's briefly walk through all the stages on the map. Again, this is not an exhaustive explanation but rather, a high-level view of this Journey to Completion pathway. When you get a glimpse of what this journey entails, you can continue to orient your mind around this pathway.

The Call

You will receive a Call to embark on this path of venturing into your unconscious and the Dreamtime.

The Calling can come either from difficult things that occur in our lives, such as the loss of a loved one, a death, a breakup, a physical illness, or mounting anxiety resulting from past wounds. It can also come from extraordinarily good things occurring, such as an ecstatic state, a new relationship, or a new job on the horizon.

Regardless of how the Calling arises, you will feel clear that you want to explore the parts of yourself that until this point have remained hidden. When you answer the Calling, you are agreeing to set out on a pathway to reclaim even more of your personal power and become a more impeccable person in your use of power.

Affirmations

Once you have recognized what is Calling you onto this adventure during this time of your life, you look for Affirmations. These Affirmations may be big or small, but they always show you that you are on the right path. It is a big undertaking to go down into your Dreamtime/the Underworld, so you want to know that it is truly the right time in your life to undertake this journey.

This is especially true when doing psychedelics. You want to make sure that you really are ready to deconstruct the mind and are in a stable enough space to do so.

An Affirmation may take the form of a friend randomly telling you about something that relates to what you are reading in this book or hearing strangers talking on the airplane about something related to your Calling. Affirmations are often "passing messengers" telling you that, yes, now is the right time for you to undertake this voyage.

Threshold Guardians

Just as there are elements that affirm you are on the right path, there are also guardians that appear to make sure that you are truly ready to step over into the Dreamtime. Threshold Guardians sit in the space between the ordinary and non-ordinary and test if it is the appropriate time to cross over.

In relation to psychedelics, this can look like your travel plans to go somewhere to do the ceremony gets messed up or new information comes to light about a substance you were planning to ingest.

Threshold Guardians are not necessarily there to stop you from going on the journey; however, they give you pause. Taking a moment to really take note of the Threshold Guardians is essential because they *foreshadow the Shadow*. This means that however the Threshold Guardians are showing up, these elements are likely to be a part of the bigger Shadow pattern that you will need to face in the Underworld.

Setting Your Intent

Setting your Intent statement is how you say yes to your Calling. Spirit gives you the Calling and then it is up to you to act and follow the Calling—to either say yes or no. Threshold Guardians will actually stop you if it is not the right time for you to tackle this Shadow pattern, and

Affirmations will come quite synchronistically across your path to let you know if it is the right time to venture into the Dreamtime. Thus, there is built into the Journey to Completion Map a natural screening process. You are literally entering into a commitment to deepen your relationship with Great Spirit, with "the realms of power," when you choose to cross this threshold and set your Intent.

You must set a clear Intent, which your guide can help you discuss and gain clarity on. This statement of purpose includes your positive desire and willingness to name and grapple with certain Shadow issues. The relationship with your guide is of utmost importance. If you are going into the altered space to examine your Shadow, then it makes sense that you cannot see certain aspects of yourself, the parts submerged in your own unconscious. Your guide can provide the necessary support to identify insights that are not accessible otherwise. After formulating a good Intent statement, you are given permission to undertake this journey.

Within the Journey to Completion, it is taught that setting an Intent always contains two parts: the positive Intent you wish to achieve (the Via Positiva) and the wounded place you are willing to explore to get the gift from it (the Via Negativa).

It is very important to name both of these aspects of the Call right from the beginning, so that when shadowy challenges do arise during the journey, you will not be shocked; rather, you will already have some familiarity with them and accept the truth that you are being guided to examine them for the purpose of bringing healing.

Via Positiva

Take a moment now to reflect on what positive Intent you hold. Ask yourself, what is it that I *must have* next in my life?
- What long-held dream for your life have you not yet accomplished that you would like to bring forth next?
- What aspect of a more meaningful, purposeful life is Calling you right now? Is it a more fulfilling work life, a co-creative love partner, or the healing of a multigenerational family wound?

- Even more to the point, who would you like to become?

When you enter the Underworld, you are not supposed to be running around in there randomly. You need to have a specific goal or reason for going into the Underworld terrain. Your clear Intent acts like a rudder on the ship of your psyche—it will help orient and remind you why you sought to go on this adventure. We go into the Underworld with a specific purpose that steers the type of encounter with our Shadow in the Underworld domain. This is the first step in beginning to link up with your Inner Guidance System.

Via Negativa

Now think about what has stopped you in the past from achieving these shifts in consciousness and gifts in your life. These are the wounded places you must explore to retrieve your lost soul parts. As noted above, the Threshold Guardians you encounter at the outset, as you get ready to enter, will often foreshadow the themes of the Shadow work you will be encountering in the Dreamtime.

Ask yourself the following questions:
- What has held you back from seeing the shifts you want in your life?
- What past lineage Shadow patterns or trauma wounds do you need to explore in order to get the gift from them? What do you think is stopping you from attaining what you want?
- Your Intent will always contain both Via Positiva and Via Negativa elements. Within the Journey to Completion, the clear Intent statement is formulated in the following way:

– **Via Positiva** – I must have this…
– **Via Negativa** – Therefore, I am willing to explore the Shadow of this… in order to receive the gift from it.

Internal Guidance System

This is the stage where you link up with your Internal Guidance System to lead you during your trek in the Underworld. A big component of this is finding your power animal through drumming journeys. This relationship with your power animal is real and intimate and will be a key element in learning to psycho-navigate within drumming journeys.

It is important to learn how to connect with your inner guidance when venturing into your psyche because it is the compass for your ship. Being able to trust that you are venturing in the right direction allows your psyche to reveal what it needs to.

When learning to follow the power animal's guidance, you are being trained to stalk your Shadow, to follow your power, rather than follow your habitual patterns of self-sabotage and leaking of power.

Studying the Shadow

Once you have connected with your Inner Guidance you are ready to take on the task of studying the Shadow. We revealed our unique system for sequestering the Shadow in its totality earlier in Chapter 5 through the Outer/Inner Shadow Chart. This technique trains you how to track within your own mind and find these lost parts. You learn how not to be tricked or sidetracked by your Shadow but rather, to stalk it and understand your own system of obscurations or defense mechanisms.

This system also teaches you how to track and notice the way your outer tormentors or triggering people are misusing their power over you. It is a double tracking modality that allows you to follow your Inner and Outer Shadow.

An Indigenous elder once told us that "the Shadow is like a slippery fish." In the phase of studying the Shadow, you are building the "net" to capture the "slippery fish" of the Shadow. It is like a Sherlock Holmes investigation within your inner world. We are our own game of Clue; we must learn to follow the clues in order to understand the role of each character.

This book will take you up to this stage of the Journey to Completion Map and help you learn how to do these important steps for working with your Shadow. The next steps come as you progress along the full Journey to Completion pathway.

Transmuting the Shadow

Once you have gone through the process of adequately naming and sequestering your Shadow material, you move on to a process of Transmutation. The Outer Shadow often contains powers we actually *need* in our lives; however, they have been either misused against us or warped within us.

Taking the powers from the Outer Shadow and transmuting them is an alchemical act of working with the energy behind the Shadow and integrating it within yourself. This process is done in a day-long ritual in which the energy of the pattern is brought into a somatic "felt sense" and the powers that your Outer Shadow held for so long are fully understood and delivered to you. This is the path of heart, so you have a right to use these tremendous powers only after you have done the healing of your wounds so that you do not misuse the power. You use these powers gained with a good heart and for the highest good of all. The Transmutation process involves somatic energy work, ritual drama therapy, and a powerful method of obtaining the gift from the Shadow that is both cognitive and somatic.

Feast in the Underworld

At this point, you have accomplished the alchemical process of facing the Shadow and harnessing its powers. You are still in the Underworld, yet a radical shift has taken place. To honor this undertaking, you will be magically presented with a "feast," or a reward. It will be specific to you, and you will recognize it as such.

For example, one client was separated from his grandmother in India for years. He hadn't been able to get in contact with her between the ages of nine and 24. Immediately after he did his Shadow work and completed this Transmutation, the grandmother in India was brought a phone and was finally able to contact him. The reward was very apropos to the healing of the wound that set the Shadow process in motion in the first place.

Practicing the Change in Perspective

Through Transmuting your Shadow an entirely new power has been embedded within you. Now the task is to practice this new way of being. Note that you are still in the Dreamtime (Underworld), and this is a time of diligently working with these new ways of being.

Opportunities will arise to test if you've truly integrated the gifts of the Shadow material. You will be faced with situations that in the past would have elicited habitual knee-jerk reactions. As the new powers take root in you, this will no longer be the case. The same potholes in the road will no longer lure you and catch you off guard.

The knowledge of the Shadow pattern gives you keen awareness and you're no longer available to interact with it in the same old vibrational alignments. You are set free to act in entirely new ways because your perception has shifted.

Threshold Guardians

Just as you faced Threshold Guardians on the way into the Underworld, you also face them on the way out. They are there to make sure that you fully receive the gifts of your quest. If you are not finished, they may stop you from coming all the way out yet. Generally, however, these Guardians are gentler than the ones you faced going into the Underworld. They may mirror ones you had going in, but this time you meet them with ease and skill.

For example, one client was going on a literal journey to come and work with me in Santa Fe, and her car broke down in the desert. The roadside assistance driver who came turned out to be a very threatening man who breached her boundaries, and she had a strong, fearful reaction and was entwined in her habitual, fearful Shadow patterns.

This was a Threshold Guardian at the beginning of her journey into the Underworld. It allowed her to see the wounded and scared places within herself. After completing her journey of Transmutation of the Shadow and practicing the Change in Perspective, she had an amazingly similar incident happen on the return journey, when her car broke down again and a tow truck came to get her. However, this time it was entirely different. She was no longer afraid, and the man who came to help her was kind and caring. This is a good example of how the Threshold Guardians will appear in a similar way at the end of the journey, but this time you experience them as assisting you in moving toward your destination of completion.

Celebration Feast

Once you have stepped back over the line that divides the Dreamtime and Ordinary Reality, your next task is to hold a Celebration Feast. Heroes of old knew the importance of sharing these voyages with the community upon their return. This step involves gathering your close community and telling them about the journey you took. Within oral traditions, the importance of verbally sharing your experiences is honored.

The act of telling what you went through aloud, to your friends and family, solidifies the changes within you. It also is a tremendous gift to everyone who hears it, because we are all interdependent. The lessons of others are very encouraging and can thus be integrated into our own lives. That is one reason why movies and novels are so important to humans. They take us on a transformational journey, and through them, our psyches can shift and we learn valuable lessons.

You will learn how important it is to share your drumming journeys, dreaming experiences, and psychedelic journeys. Contained within the act of sharing is a form of integration. By writing down your experiences and telling them aloud to those you trust, you are organizing your narrative. In the act of telling the story, you gain new insights and solidify the lessons learned.

The Clean-Up

The final step in your journey is to do the work of cleaning up. This is where the structures of Ordinary Reality are shifted and adjusted to match your new more integrated self. Having embarked on this journey and gone through all the stages, you really do come out of it as a new configuration of energy.

The world you are stepping back into may no longer match who you've become. Your job, close relationships, or living environment may no longer be a fit, like the proverbial round peg trying to fit into the square hole. This does not mean that you will be leaving these situations or people necessarily; however, the external structures will shift to match the new internal state you are living in. The structures of reality will actually become more harmonious and sustainable with whom you've become.

The Journey to Completion method takes you into the full process of a deep encounter with the energy systems of your particular Shadow dynamics, then teaches you the transmutation process, which is thorough and brings about a complete pattern shift. The warrior moves you discover in that process are then carried out and practiced in your Ordinary Reality life for a period of time to systematically integrate them. Then the whole circle of the journey is completed with a Celebration Feast, where you share with your close community the elements of your journey to the Underworld and back, having attained and integrated the gifts of the Shadow. This final stage of the communal sharing and closing the alchemical container carefully is an essential part of successful Shadow work that must not be ignored.

Now that you have seen the Journey to Completion Map, you will understand the parts we are referencing as we teach you about drumming journeys, dreamwork, and psychedelics. Throughout, we may reference sections of this map. If you ever feel lost, return to this section, and study the map once again.

12

Three Modes of Entering Altered States of Consciousness

The Dreamtime and Lucid Dreaming, Drumming-Induced Journey, and Psychedelic-Induced Journey

Having seen the full map of the Journey to Completion, you can now begin to understand that there is a step-by-step progression into the psyche. Through the systematic practices of shamanic drumming journeys and lucid dreaming, you can take the first steps on the ancient pathway into gaining psychonavigation expertise. Bringing together these modalities and applying the lessons from them to psychedelic journeys creates a holistic approach to learning the terrain of our minds.

The three methods for working with the psyche may seem vastly different, but each one perfectly complements and builds upon the other. With all three, you strengthen the skill of working with your mind.

Ancient traditional ways teach that we must first train the mind to become more skilled at navigating altered states before taking an entheogen, or plant medicine. Drum-induced and lucid dream–induced trance states offer a step-by-step approach to learning advanced psychonavigational skills.

Looking at the Journey to Completion Map in the previous chapter, you can see that these stages progress sequentially. Once you've answered the Call to enter the psyche and passed the Threshold Guardians, drumming journeys help you connect with your Internal Guidance system and meet your ally. Working with your dreams and engaging in lucid dreaming practices not only helps you become more conscious of the Dreamtime but also helps you begin to study the Shadow.

Psychedelic journeys also provide a prime opportunity to study the Shadow, because the Shadow almost always arises within them. As the Psychedelic Renaissance continues to grow in popularity, numerous books are being published about the psychedelic journey. These books cover a wide range of topics. They often focus on how to hold space for a journey for another and how to integrate afterwards.

Working with a facilitator or therapist leading up to the journey is also discussed. We will teach you how to create a container that extends beyond that short time leading up to the journey and a little while after. The container that is outlined in this book is a pathway you walk for your entire lifetime.

In a culture enthralled by extremes, many people take higher and higher doses of psychedelics in hopes of reaching the outermost limits of consciousness, or thinking they can skip over certain stages of healing. Reaching for the stars is fine, yet sometimes this fast-paced method leads to deepening fractures within the psyche.

This is especially true when one is not taking the time to integrate information that has been revealed within the extreme altered states. In fact, sometimes this chase can originate from not wanting to slow down and look at the wounds in the first place. Serving as another tool for actually numbing the pain, psychedelic use can become especially deluding when mixed with an attitude of spiritual superiority.

Through experiencing the subtle, you will be ready to handle the heightened experiences that come your way with more skillful means, understanding, accuracy, and finesse. This book teaches you how to prepare your mind for altered states. There is an ancient art form to psychonavigation. Through practice, you learn to gradually and accurately understand how the map of the mind works.

PART 2

Drumming Journeys

13

Entering Trance States through Sound Induction

The defining quality of shamanism is the ecstatic experience derived from self-induced trance states, most often reached through drumming.

—LAYNE REDMOND, When the Drummers Were Women

Working with drumming-induced trance journeys is an ancient way of training the voyager in how to navigate the mind. Learning how to enter a trance state from waking reality is a wonderful first step. You realize that you have access to altered states inside you at any moment you choose.

The book *When the Drummers Were Women* by Layne Redmond contains the author's extensive cross-cultural research about the history of drumming and how civilizations have used it to alter states of consciousness. During the course of her studies of communities around the world, Redmond came upon the Greek word *gymnosophism*, which refers to the techniques Egyptians used in the pursuit of expanded consciousness. These techniques included visualization, rhythmic breathing, and chanting to rhythmic accompaniment. She notes that it's similar to many of the yogic practices of Hinduism.

Rhythmic drumming to expand consciousness has been practiced traditionally throughout the world, from the Celts of the British Isles to the Sami of Norway to Mongolian shamans. Trace your ancestry back far enough and you will probably find music being used as a key tool for psychological healing. Although in our modern world we may have been disconnected from this practice, when given the correct techniques, most people can learn this skill.

The steady drumbeat carries you from waking reality into the unknown spaces of the subconscious. Once fully immersed in the trance state you learn how to find your power animal, which symbolically anchors you to your strong inner guidance system (your inner compass).

Fig. 7: The Ascent into the Dreamtime (Nisha Burton, 2024)

The terrain encountered in drumming journeys is not only composed of your own subconscious domain; you also enter into the vast collective unconscious. Having led literally thousands of people in drumming journeys, we have found that there are similar spaces and experiences that journeyers discover, no matter the geographical location of the person.

Remarkably, humans all over the world visit a similar inner landscape. This implies that there is a place that exists, a geography of the domains of the Underworld, that remains the same across cultures. New neural pathways of communication between your conscious and subconscious mind are mapped, and your Ordinary Reality and Dreamtime sync up. The drumbeat helps you find the ladder within you on which you can ascend and descend.

The Ancient Pathway of Initiation through Drumming Journeys

Of all the things a shaman does, the drumming-induced trance is the most often discussed. It is frequently viewed as the ultimate experience in shamanism. Through the steady beat of the drum, a link with everyday reality is created so that the shaman can safely return to Ordinary Reality. When a person came to them with a psychical or mental ailment, healers would go into a trance to seek the root cause of their client's issue.

To accurately understand what you encounter in the trance state takes time and is a level of accomplishment that comes after witnessing hundreds of journeys. To then be able to ethically guide another psyche without misusing power over the voyager is a level of mastery in an advanced skill set. Practice, in this case, makes perfect.

Every time you enter this state, think of it as a mini hero's journey. Much like the Greek goddess Persephone, the journeyer goes down into the Underworld to bring back the hidden treasures that exist where many dare not venture. Going into a trance state allows you to step past the barriers of the waking mind that hide your deeper core issues. There are gateways that your mind sets up for its own protection that must be carefully met and understood all along the way.

It is no secret that although plant medicines can be deeply healing, they also carry with them the danger of psychological and even physical harm. The ability to navigate a trance is essential and takes strong mental conditioning. That is why we emphasize that a trance state may be achieved without any substances through the drumming journey. It is a practice of self-hypnosis that alters the brain's theta waves through this auditory driving of the brain. However, because it is coming from within, the individual risks of psychological or physical harm are greatly reduced here.

In his book *Psychedelic Integration: Psychotherapy for Non-Ordinary States of Consciousness*, Marc Aixala states, "Mindfulness mixed with psychedelics makes it easier to enter and stay in those states." As you get better at navigating altered realms in non-psychedelic altered states, you will find that you have more successful and transformational psychedelic journeys when you do use the plant medicines.

The one who beats the drum is not just simply beating the drum; they are transmitting energy through the drum that opens a doorway, a portal, through which those listening can enter and find themselves in the domain of the Dreamtime.

Before the drumming journey starts, the guide will give you instructions about how to follow the pathway to take you down into the Dreamtime. Once the drumming starts, the guide no longer speaks and you follow the outlined pathway down and then see what naturally arises. You open your mind as an information receptacle until a specific message is received from the spirit world. Once the message is received and the messenger is acknowledged, you come out of the trance and share the journey.

Although you have a guide for the drumming journey, the shamanic trance is not focused on anyone telling you what to think, as is the case in guided meditation or hypnosis; rather, you are taught to follow an ancient set of guidelines. In that manner, you are traveling within your psyche at your own pace and in your own timing, not being pushed or dominated by an external other. You are actively learning to follow your own inner guidance system.

The instructions are a road map, yet you are the one navigating the map in your own way, in your own timing. This allows you to develop your navigational skills based on your natural proclivities and talents. That is why the Huichol marakame call this drum-induced trance journey Gathering Your Power. It is your spiritual power that you are seeking; it is your soul retrieval, which only you can do.

14

Your Brain on Drumming –
The Science behind the Drumming-Induced Trance

Not only has drumming been verified through the ages by many Indigenous cultures but now scientists are catching up and seeing how impactful drumming is on the brain. It's common knowledge that humans have two hemispheres in our brain, the right and the left. These two regions rule different functions in our processing abilities.

Our mind is constantly oscillating between the two regions throughout the day. The right and left hemispheres operate in different modes and rhythms. For example, one side could be generating alpha waves while the other is generating beta ones.

In *When the Drummers Were Women,* Layne Redmond explores how the two hemispheres of the brain can synchronize in rhythm when in states of deep meditation or intense creativity. This same effect can be created through rhythmic sound. It produces a state of mind that is a unified whole-brain functioning called *hemispheric synchronization*.

When hemispheric synchronization takes place, one enters a state of clarity, heightened awareness, and a lack of separation. You are no longer limited to drawing from one side, then the other, and instead, can draw from both hemispheres simultaneously. When hemispheric synchronization is combined with alpha brainwaves the feeling of expanded mental powers has been reported. Thus, higher states of consciousness could be correlated to the synchronization of these two hemispheres.

As Layne Redmond writes, "Many ancient religious practices seem to have originated in attempts to induce the transcendent experience of hemispheric synchronization. Chanting rhythmically while gazing at geometric figures—like the tantric combination of mantra and yantra—facilitates synchronization by simultaneously engaging the verbal skills of one hemisphere with the visual skills of the other."

Although cultures have been experimenting with these technologies for a long time, scientists have now labeled this powerful ancient trance induction method as *auditory driving*. The speed and rhythm in which the drum is played can directly influence the human body.

Entrainment is a phenomenon found throughout nature, whereby two or more vibrating bodies will come into similar rhythmic cycles. For example, as discovered by Dutch scientist Christian Huygens in 1665, two pendulums placed near one another will eventually start ticking in unison. Since the brain is primed to *entrain* with rhythmic cycles when the steady beat of the drum is applied, the brain wave frequency can shift from one state into another. Our minds are literally primed to go into trance states, and all we need to do is apply the correct stimuli.

The Effect of Drumming on Brain Wave Frequencies

There are four basic levels of human awareness, each represented by different brain frequency ranges. Let's explore what each brain wave frequency feels like, from the deepest to the most alert:

1. The slowest brain wave state is *delta*, which occurs at frequencies of up to 4 hertz (a hertz is one cycle per second). This state is associated with unconsciousness and the deepest level of sleep.
2. The second slowest brain wave state is *theta*, which occurs between 4 and 8 hertz. This state is where hallucinations and imagery take place and is the state we enter when we meditate or go on a drumming journey. Theta waves are linked to vivid imagery, dreams, and creativity. The transition between alpha waves to theta waves is when *hypnagogia* occurs. Hypnogogic experiences are the hallucinations that happen just as you are falling asleep. This state is related to lucid dreaming, sleep paralysis, and body jerks.

3. The third brain wave state is *alpha*, which occurs between 8 and 13 hertz. Alpha is considered a relaxed yet alert state, where we are aware of our external world but are deeply relaxed. This state can happen when closing the eyes and relaxing but still awake.
4. The fourth brain wave state is *beta*. Beta occurs between 13 and 30 hertz and is our normal, wakeful state of being.

When listening to a repetitive, steady drum beat, our brains begin to pulsate in time with the beat. It has been well established that sound produces changes in a person's brain waves, especially at the theta level. This is what we refer to as the "auditory driving" of the brain.

When beating the drum, the guide will drum in a steady, monotonous rhythm. Gradually they increase in tempo, bringing the voyager into an altered state of consciousness. A drumming frequency range of 4–7 cycles per second is generally viewed as producing the desired altered state. Thus, the person beating the drum is producing both the container and the driving force for the journey.

In this sense, the guide and her drumming are the anchors to everyday reality for the journeyer. As the journeyer drifts into theta brain waves, images cross their mind and they enter into what Michael Harner, the grandfather of contemporary shamanism, refers to as the Shamanic State of Consciousness (SSC).

When successful, the imagery of a shamanic journey and the rituals that are part of the experience are immensely powerful. The marriage of this imagery and ritual has become the focal point of much research because the profound psychological impact that can take place.

In the past 30 years, it's been a real boon to have scientific validation of the true efficaciousness of spiritual practices like drum-induced trance states. For better or worse, the "proof" of scientists validating these ancient truths can be helpful in legitimizing them in Western culture. In addition, when we understand that these ancient technologies are having a "real" impact on our psychological selves, we can trust their value.

15

Healing Effects of Drum Journeys

After drumming journeys, participants come back to Ordinary Reality expressing wonder, excitement, and even euphoria. The credit belongs to the drum, the magical sacred drum, wielded by a skilled guide, which has the extraordinary power to touch something deep and powerful within. The drum resonates with the part of us that knows nothing of cell phones, texts, and deadlines. The part of us to which the drum speaks knows inner peace, self-expression, and our very basic life force, our heartbeat.

Nada Yoga is the yoga of sound. In this ancient practice, music is used as a spiritual technology because it is considered that ultimate reality resides in vibration. The physical world is a manifestation of different frequencies of this root vibrational energy. Redmond states, the goal of Nada Yoga is communion with this pulsing vibration behind all sound—the *bindu*—the point out of which everything arises. The heartbeat behind all heartbeats.

We enter this life entrained to the heartbeat of our mothers in the womb, are sustained in life by our own heartbeat, and are synchronized with the rhythmic heartbeat of all that surrounds us. The drumbeat sounds very similar to a steady heartbeat. It serves as a mechanism to connect us to the universal heartbeat, and thereby, go into the depths of the unknown (and our psyche).

Studies have shown that drumming can help improve mood, reduce anxiety, and enhance cognitive function in Alzheimer's patients. Furthermore, it can help improve social skills, communication, motor coordination, emotional expression, and nonverbal self-expression for children with autism. The benefits of drumming are being applied in numerous settings.

Drumming has also been used to aid emotionally disturbed teens, as well as by large corporations to help employees focus attention and improve their spirit. Scientific studies are now showing that drumming, even for brief periods, changes a person's brainwave patterns, dramatically reducing stress.

In a 1978 treatise, Joseph Bearwalker Wilson provides an excellent discussion of a theory of trance. He has said: "The shaman uses the trance state to fine-tune his senses. Using those enhanced senses, the shaman then is able to mind-travel to the spiritual world, to enter a different dimension."

Our Western culture tends to emphasize sight over the other senses, so we are conditioned to expect visual imagery in the trance state, but the messages can come through any of the senses. When we lead people on drumming journeys, they sometimes express frustration at not being able to see anything the first few times. Thus, we always encourage journeyers to open all of their senses when they enter the drum-induced imaginal realms. The sense of sight can tend to dominate, yet it is also essential to pay attention to the sense of hearing, touch, taste, smell, and spatial felt sense, because the messages from the Dreamtime can come through any of the senses, not just visual imagery.

For example, one student returned from the underworld and reported she had not really "seen" anything. But as she was questioned further and encouraged to speak more about her journey, she reported that she had this sensation that she was looking out of each side of her head, not straight ahead. She felt she was very large, had a sensation of floating in space, and her skin felt hyper-sensitive.

As we discussed it further, it became apparent that she had entered fully into feeling herself inside of the whale and was sensorially aware of the ways a whale might see, move, and feel in its own skin. This merging with the power animal usually occurs at a later stage of journeying, but she had felt all of these remarkable sensations of being one with her power animal early on. It is important not to discount information coming to us from multi-sensory input.

If you have this roadblock of not visually seeing things in your journey state, remember to connect with your other senses. Ask yourself, what do I hear, smell, or feel right now? You may be surprised to feel soft fur brushing across your cheek, hear the flutter of wings past your ear, or feel the dampness of the cool skin of a snake curl around your arm. Within the drumming journey trance states your senses will heighten, and you will be trained to feel so much more than you thought possible. You are being schooled in trusting the body and the senses and not shrinking back in fear. In the Dreamtime, there is nothing to fear.

This brings up the fact that blockages to experiencing the effects of a drumming journey can also come from our cultural conditioning around imagination and what is real.

As Robert Spencer states in *The Craft of the Warrior*: "It turns out that we adopt certain ways of perceiving based on experience and beliefs that determine what kinds of sensory stimuli we allow into awareness. Essentially, we interpret our sensory data through filters of our beliefs and experiences. If we do not believe in something, chances are we will not perceive it. If we perceive it, we will interpret it in a way that is consistent with our belief structure."

Being open to the profound journeys you can take within a drumming trance may require letting go of the belief that what you are sensing is not "real." Check in with yourself if you are struggling to enter into the imaginal Dreamtime realms to see if your perception is being unconsciously limited. Recognize where outdated feelings, thoughts, and perceptions are limiting your current construction of reality.

16

Four Stages of Entering a Trance or Dream

Generally speaking, there are four basic levels of a shamanic trance. Stages might be the more appropriate term. Well-practiced and experienced shamans can go directly into the fourth stage of the trance. However, when you are beginning your voyage into the psyche using drumming, you will find that these stages are the ones you encounter. It is helpful to know ahead of time what to expect so you can recognize each stage as it passes.

- **The first stage** is common among beginners. You have a sense of being physically relaxed, even drowsy. There is a tendency to just stare off into the darkness of your closed eyelids, unseeing. The pulse rate slows.
- **The second stage** produces a feeling that the whole body is heavy; a sense of detachment occurs. There may be visual illusions, and you are aware that you are in a trance.
- **The third stage** brings full recognition that you are in a trance. Here, you may actually choose a part of your body not to feel pain. There is a greater sensitivity to temperature changes as well as to atmospheric pressure. There will be a loss of voluntary motion and reaction to external stimuli.
- **The fourth and final stage** is where the shamanic trance is deepest. Control over several body functions, such as heartbeat, blood pressure, and body temperature, becomes possible. Memories will be recalled, and age regression may come into play. There will be a feeling of lightness, of floating or flying. Visual and auditory hallucinations are possible while at this stage of the trance.

Client Example of Going into a Drumming Trance

Closing my eyes, I began listening to the steady beat of the drum. The drum's rhythm filled my senses. I could feel it pulsing into the deepest recesses of my being.

As the sound of the drum bounced off the walls of the small, bare room, my ears started playing tricks on me. I heard one voice, then another. They spoke to me in a language without words, just vibration. Soon I heard more drums, more voices singing. Next, a chorus of angels. After a while, I no longer heard the drum's beat but felt it in my body as my temples pulsated to their incessant rhythm.

My body grew heavy. I felt like I was being pushed into the ground, while at the same time being lifted, drawn out of my body by the beat of the drum. This sensation faded as I rode the rhythm into a world much different than my own.

It is in the fourth and final stage that the drum journeyer travels into the Underworld and receives instructions regarding the Quest. We have found that there are stark similarities between the stages of drumming journeys and a specific technique of going from the waking state directly into a lucid dream. When transitioning from the waking mind directly into the lucid state (an advanced lucid dream technique) your body and mind take a similar journey as the one we just reviewed.

In *The Art of Dreaming*, the first task that Castaneda is given by Don Juan is to transition from being awake right into lucid sleep without losing awareness in the process. Don Juan states that the first threshold of dreaming that one must cross is to be aware of the particular sensation before deep sleep, which is a pleasant heaviness and inability to open one's eyes.

Castaneda asks Don Juan if there are any steps to follow or ways to become aware that he is falling asleep, and Don Juan just says no. This seems to be the teaching method of Don Juan throughout his work with Castaneda, to simply give the task without much instruction and leave

Castaneda to figure it out himself. Don Juan hopes that Castaneda will step through the portal from waking reality into the Dreamtime simply by intending to do so.

As well as using strong Intent, there is another way to strengthen the muscle of transitioning from a waking state into a dreamlike state—through the beat of the drum. Practicing the technique of drumming journeys not only gives you the ability to work within the domain of the drumming realms but also primes your consciousness for this advanced dreaming technique. Notice the similarities between the stages of entering the drumming journey trance and entering the lucid dream from waking consciousness.

Four Stages of Entering Your Lucid Dream from Waking Consciousness

- STAGE 1: *You are lying awake in your bed.* You hold the focus of staying mentally awake while letting your body fall asleep. You are physically relaxed and stare off into the darkness of your closed eyelids.
- STAGE 2: *You feel like your whole body is heavy.* You can focus your mind on contracting and relaxing each muscle group in your body, from your toes to your head in sequential order. At some point, your body should no longer feel able to move.
- STAGE 3: *Hypnagogic imagery begins to form.* You may see flashing lights, geometric patterns, images of people or places from your day, and so on. In this stage, you might also hear hypnagogic sounds like knocking and crashing. It is essential that you remain focused on staying awake while falling asleep. This is the hardest part, because the mind will tend to fall directly into the dream at this point without retaining lucidity. It may take many tries before you are able to successfully cross into the Dreamtime fully lucid. But it is possible! Don't give up.

- **STAGE 4:** *You pass into the Dreamtime with full lucidity.* Many times, you will see the dream forming in front of you while still lucid. You feel elation during this fourth and final stage because you have successfully made the journey between Ordinary Reality and the Dreamtime while staying "awake." Similar to a drum-induced trance journey, you may experience a feeling of lightness, of floating or flying. If you can transition into the dream without losing the lucid awareness that you are dreaming, you will become fully immersed in a lucid dream.

Stephen LaBerge is a pioneering lucid dream researcher and teacher. In his book, *Exploring the World of Lucid Dreaming,* he names this technique of entering the dream from a wakeful state the "Hypnogogic Imagery Technique." He describes a similar practice of relaxing the body, noticing the imagery that comes up as you begin to fall asleep, and then letting yourself be drawn into the dream.

According to LaBerge, the most difficult part of this practice is the final stage, when you allow yourself to be drawn into the dream while staying aware that you are dreaming. He states, "The challenge is to develop a delicate vigilance and unobtrusive observer perspective from which you let yourself be drawn into the dream."

The "delicate vigilance" that LaBerge writes about is the same skill that one develops within drumming journeys.

NISHA'S Experience Entering the Dreamtime from a Waking State

I first read about this technique in LaBerge's book and then also encountered a similar practice of going from wakefulness to dreams in my Tibetan Dream Yoga studies. Although this is a challenging and somewhat advanced technique for lucid dreaming, I was able to accomplish it quite early on in my lucid dreaming journey.

FOUR STAGES OF ENTERING A TRANCE OR DREAM

Having been raised in the tradition of drumming journeys, I was able to harness the drum trance induction practice to help transition successfully from waking reality to the Dreamtime. I noticed the familiar sensations (which I had come to know so well in drumming journeys) while falling asleep. Knowing what to expect at each stage, I held my attention all the way into the Dreamtime.

I lay down in bed and set the Intent that tonight would be the night that I transitioned directly from being awake to lucid sleep. My mind began to flutter around as it often does when getting ready to fall asleep. Instead of letting it think random thoughts, I focused on feeling the sensations in my body.

Steadily, my body became more and more relaxed and heavy, until it felt like I could no longer move. This was exciting because I knew it meant I was getting ready to transition into the next stage. Knowing that, I remained relaxed and let the hypnagogic imagery arise without getting overly drawn into or distracted by it.

In my peripheral vision (with my eyes closed) I saw various geometric patterns forming like fractals surrounding me. With pointed attention, I continued to stare ahead into the blackness. I was amazed that it was working. I could actually feel my body falling fully asleep without "blacking out" into the dream as usual.

Finally, I saw a dream form in front of me. It was like going through a wormhole and seeing a scene at the end of the tunnel. In this case, it was a city street. I arrived in the dream landscape fully lucid, amazed by what I had just accomplished.

This is just the beginning of seeing how interrelated lucid dreaming and drum trance journeys are. In fact, training in the skill of going into a trance through drumming will prime you to be able to accomplish the challenging task of entering a lucid dream from a state of wakefulness.

Pointing out the similarities suggests a larger truth: There is a clear pathway that humans can take into the psyche. Across cultures, this pathway has been documented, and you can come to know it first hand by engaging in these practices yourself. Of course, each person will encounter elements of the journey in slightly different ways; however, the underlying experience described above is universal.

17

Where We Travel in Drumming Journeys

Maps hold power because they name where things are placed, and those that know how to read them can find the buried treasure. In the context of colonization, maps were crucial in describing the New World, providing European settlers with a sense of control and ownership. Colonizers wielded the map as a means of control and displacement.

ALTAJ-KIZSI SÁMÁNDOB
(TUNGUR) RAJZOLATA

Fig. 8: Drawings on an Altai-Kizhi Samandob (drum head)

Indigenous maps often included elements absent in modern geographical maps, such as cosmology, mythology, and practical advice. As a result, Indigenous maps may hold spiritual significance and require interpretation by a shaman or medicine person, often conducted in a ceremonial context.

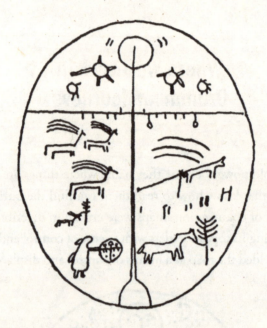

Fig. 9: Altai Shaman Drum with the Skin of a Horse on a Rod

NORMA'S Research of Maps on Drum Heads

A few years ago, I saw a photo of an ancient head of a drum on which there were painted stick-figure-like drawings. Instantly I recognized that this was something of great significance. It was clear that a voyager had made these drawings as a map on their drum head after going into altered trance states. The head of the drum had become an illustrated journal of their Dreamtime geography, thus mapping the unique psychonavigation of their inner world terrain.

Some years later, I came upon a study carried out by female anthropologists at Colorado College who also thought these drum heads were fascinating. They collected a series of ancient images drawn on reindeer hide drum heads from the Sami culture. They found that the drum images were actually maps that held a pictographic cosmology within them that extended beyond literal and psychical spaces.

When viewed in light of the numerous journeys I have embarked upon and led people on over the years, the pictographs on the drum heads made so much sense. I recognized each illustration on the drums because I had been to these exact places, and so had my clients. It dawned on me that a marvelous truth was being revealed here: These same Dreamtime places were visited by ancient psychonauts as well as by us in current times; therefore, the collective unconscious is a storehouse of similar places not only across vast geographical zones but also eons of time.

When a voyager returns to ordinary consciousness from their drum-induced trance, their journey is elucidated in the conversations I have with the person. The insights garnered from hearing about so many journeys over the last 40 years help me orient clients around what collective landscapes they might be experiencing.

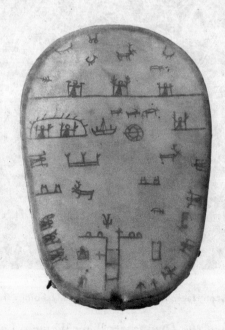

Fig. 10: Sami Drum, probably from Lule Lappmark

In their global travels and immersive studies of Indigenous societies, cultural scientists and archaeologists like Joseph Campbell[6] and Victor Turner[7] saw certain universal patterns in the shamanic journey into the psyche. In our own first-hand studies with Indigenous elders, we have also found that similar maps exist within many traditions.

From the Huichol of central Mexico; the Zuni, Navajo, and Tewa in New Mexico; the Lakota and Northern Cheyenne; the Hoopa of California; and the Haida of the Pacific Northwest to the Sami of Norway and Siberian shamans, these ancient maps of consciousness reveal that there are three basic realms in which humans travel in altered dimensions: the Underworld, the Upper World, and the Middle World. These aren't physical places but rather, archetypal and energetic domains—zones of consciousness and geographies of the inner cosmos.

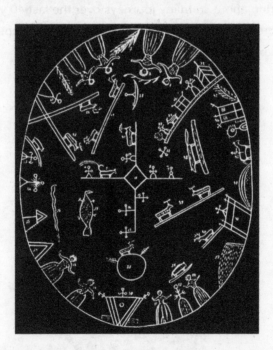

Fig. 11: Nordic Sami Naero Runic Shaman Drum Mythology from Friis, 1871

In her book *When the Drummers Were Women*, Layne Redmond confirms that throughout various cultures, healers have used the drum to journey into three worlds. Through the beat of the drum, skilled shamans can travel between the worlds at will.

Redmond goes on to state, "The interconnectedness of these realms is universally represented by the Tree of Life, which is rooted in the underworld, bears fruit on earth, and reaching with its topmost branches into the heavens."

The Tree of Life is one of the symbols for the axis mundi. Thus, the beat of the drum is facilitating the shaman's consciousness in moving up and down the axis mundi, the ladder, or passageway between the worlds.

The Three Worlds

- The **Middle World (or Earth)** is where we work and raise our families. This is the space where we inhabit our bodies in our waking lives.
- The **Upper World** is the invisible domain of our destiny and our spirit (the heavens). Here, we meet powerful human-like guides. Released from the limitations of the human world, we can achieve what seem like superpowers in these palaces of light. This is where you venture to find your highest destiny.
- The **Underworld**, where the record of all human history is held, is the realm of the soul. The Underworld is vast. Carl Jung said it is in the Underworld that we tap into not only our own vast Dreamtime psyche but also the collective unconscious. You go to the Underworld to retrieve your lost soul parts, because that's where your childhood and former lifetimes reside.

The Shadow is a significant issue in Underworld journeys. Most journeys to the Underworld will involve an encounter with your Shadow. Carl Jung famously said, "The unconscious is satisfied with the symbolic realms." Much of our Shadow material is therefore sent into the symbolic realms of the unconscious to be dealt with. When you journey into the Underworld, you will encounter the Shadow in many symbolic ways in order to process your Shadow patterns and past traumas.

This work must be done first, before venturing into the Upper or Middle worlds. Why? Because in the Underworld, you must surrender and be cleansed or healed from your trauma wounds and defense mechanisms so that you are able to hold the power that comes with the Upper World ethics and the right use of power.

Only with considerable Shadow work under your belt are you ready to venture into the Upper World, where you learn to embody your vast potentialities of power with responsibility. Finally, you venture into the Middle World. This is the last stage of the journey, because when you enter the Middle World through a shamanic journey it is different than being in it in everyday life.

Coming into the Middle World through a trance state, it is possible to alter time and space realities, so with proper preparation, your history and the future can actually be remedied. That should only be done with utmost care and impeccability and therefore this journey to the Middle World is saved until you are ready to hold that level of power.

Knowing this pathway of progression is important. It is a dependable way to work with the landscapes of non-Ordinary Reality. Interestingly, psychedelics, like mushrooms, often take you into the Underworld as well; therefore, the more you know about how to work with this Underworld realm through drumming trance states the more capable you will be at identifying and navigating the Underworld when you encounter it in a plant medicine journey.

From our studies, we have found that you can go to similar worlds through lucid dreaming as you do through drumming journeys.

Exploring the Three Realms within Lucid Dreaming

When you learn how to identify these realms through drumming journeys you are better equipped to also recognize them in the dream state and orient yourself accordingly. Lucid dreams that take place in the Upper World are ones that involve celestial beings, amazing otherworldly landscapes, ornate palaces, or flying outside our atmosphere into the cosmos, and other destinations. Upper World lucid dreams are exhilarating, and you often wake up from them feeling transformed. As with drumming journeys, Upper World lucid explorations are spaces in which you encounter beings of power and feelings of tremendous personal empowerment. You see what you are capable of beyond the limitations of human form.

Generally, lucid dreaming doesn't cause a detachment from waking life, even though some people worry about that. However, if you are using lucid dreaming as a tool of escapism, going to the Upper World realms repeatedly could begin to cause a fixation on lucid dreaming above all else. That is why, similar to drumming journeys, you need to do your Shadow work and understand how to use power with impeccability when repeatedly visiting the Upper World in your lucid dreams.

NISHA'S Example of an Upper World Journey in a Lucid Dream

I got up in the middle of the night, and the light was off. I tried to turn it on. It wouldn't switch on; none of them would. I went back to bed but then got back up and tried it again. I was puzzled at first but then had the thought that I might be dreaming. I jumped up and sure enough, I floated! I was very happy.

I called out for my dragon ally, who I had connected with in other dreams, to come help me. I felt his presence with me, and I flew up into the solar system, whizzing past stars and other spacey configurations. I told the dragon I wanted to go beyond all that, to see what was further. I was in these wild fractals of light and color, flying through them.

I asked to see him, and he laughed and told me that I was in him. Then he reversed my flight to have me see, as I pulled further back, that all the fractals and colors I was traveling through made up his face. I was amazed.

He took me to a planet filled with dragons. They all appeared in a variety of shapes and sizes—some were long like him, some short and thick, some huge. It was amazing to have such a fantastical journey and is a good example of what Upper World lucid dream journeys can be like.

Another place that lucid dreaming will take you is to the Underworld. This often manifests as lucid dreams that are more frightening, deal with past traumas, involve animals, are recurring situations, and so on.

Similar to drumming journeys, in Underworld lucid dreams you have a profound opportunity to create real and lasting healing within your psyche by doing your Shadow integration work. In fact, once you become lucid, you can even choose to deal with nightmarish situations within your dream in an empowered and healed way. While lucid, you know that nothing can hurt your physical body. There is no death in the dream realms; therefore, you can face your fears in a whole new way.

Some ways you can seek out healing in the Underworld during lucid dreaming include:

- Summoning your inner child to speak with you about how current issues relate to past childhood wounds
- Entering a recurring nightmare or situation with full lucidity and resolving it once and for all
- Seeking out an animal ally to guide you in the dreamworlds.

We dedicate an entire chapter to train you how to deal with nightmares and challenging recurring dreams to help support you in this quest. It's always a good idea to have support from a therapist in your waking life while dealing with fears, especially past traumas, in your Dreamtime.

Finally, we have found that the Middle World has striking similarities to Out of Body Experiences (OBEs) or Astral Projection.

If you often become conscious while your body is still asleep (also known as sleep paralysis), you can enter the OBE state more easily by pulling your dream body out of your sleeping body. Once you are in the

OBE, you are in a reality much closer to Ordinary Reality than most lucid dreaming experiences. You'll often find yourself in your room. It may be slightly different—have an extra door or glow in a bluish color, for example—yet still feel very much like being in your known physical reality. You can do things in the OBE that you couldn't do in your waking body, such as walk through walls and float, but most often, the experiences you have in the OBE will be closer to your waking reality.

Example of a Middle World Out of Body Experience from NISHA

I woke up in bed but could tell my physical body wasn't fully awake. It was in a sleep paralysis state. I knew it was a chance to have an OBE.

I started to pull myself up, and it felt so real that I wasn't sure if maybe my physical body really was moving. I put my hands out in front of me and flipped them a few times, and they were static and dissolving. This reassured me that I was still dreaming and gave me certainty that I was going out of body.

I pulled myself up out of bed. I wasn't sure exactly what to do. I was in my bedroom, and it looked almost exactly like my bedroom in waking reality, except that there were two mirrors on the wall in front of me instead of one. I was nervous about looking at the mirrors because, from afar, I could see a shadowy figure in them.

Deciding to be brave, I stepped close to one of the mirrors. I saw my face. It was bright, even though the room was dark, and had a bluish glow. It was like my physical body but also more etheric, and I could see blue energy flowing through it.

I smiled at myself then went over to the far window in my room. I floated through the screen into the night. I looked up at the sky, and there were trillions of stars, many more than I had ever seen. I decided to fly up to them.

18

The Underworld

Drumming journeys invariably lead to the Underworld as the initial destination. The question of why this journey must commence there often arises, particularly in Western Christian culture, which equates the Underworld with Hell.

It's essential to clarify that the Underworld is not synonymous with Hell. Instead, it represents the depths of our psyche, akin to the deep unconscious, where our Shadow resides.

Aspects of ourselves we've shunned or wounds too painful to confront lie dormant in the Underworld; thus, descending into the Underworld can evoke fear and resistance: it serves as a repository for our unresolved issues, making it daunting to revisit them. The fundamental reason for journeying into the Underworld is the voluntary surrender required to delve into our trauma wounds, Shadow complexities, and defense mechanisms. This surrender is essential for genuine and enduring healing.

What exactly are we surrendering to? It's the deconstruction of our defense mechanisms. When we do this, we stop denying and evading what needs acknowledgment and reconciliation.

If we avoid confronting and addressing our Shadow, we're likely to mishandle power. Our ego and external judgments can become stumbling blocks. Trauma often leads to the development of defensive mechanisms initially meant for protection but eventually turning dysfunctional. For instance, someone who suffered childhood abuse might unknowingly adopt dominating and harsh parenting traits, despite their aversion to such behavior. The Shadow has the capacity to manifest in various detrimental behaviors, contrary to our well-being.

The motivation for individuals to embark on the journey of healing their Shadows stems from the realization that they continuously cycle through dysfunctional patterns. The weight of these shadowy behaviors becomes intolerable, and it seems as though there's no respite from recurring situations, triggers, and stressful individuals.

While this can evoke feelings of hopelessness, there's a clear and structured approach to confront and address the Shadow. Essential to this process is delving into the Underworld, where Shadow integration work unfolds.

In chapter 11, which outlines the Journey to Completion map, in formulating your Intent, you were directed to clarify both your *via positiva* and *via negativa*. Take a moment to contemplate what that Intent statement was. It holds the power you seek as you venture into the Underworld of your psyche through drumming journeys.

Indigenous teachings perceive the Underworld as a lush, dark, and fertile womb-like space. It's where the seed of our potential takes its initial steps toward conscious realization. This realm is akin to what the Inca described as Pachamama, the nurturing mother from whom we originate and to whom we will ultimately return. The Great Mother dwells within the nurturing soil of the earth, embodying the essence of Gaia herself.

Much like seeds must be planted in the earth in order to grow, the Underworld symbolizes a living, nourishing sanctuary where we can seek restoration and renewal. After all, our bodies are of the earth.

As Western culture distanced itself from its pagan, earth-centric origins, the predominant religions of the West—Judeo-Christian, Greco-Roman, and Islamic—began to depict the lower world as the realm of burial, associating it with concepts of Hell, Suffering, and even the dominion of a Devil. The earth ceased to be revered as our nurturing mother and instead, became a feared realm to avoid. This shift instilled a collective fear of darkness, femininity, and the unconscious in Western culture. However, adopting a non-dualistic perspective reveals that Heaven (representing the logical mind) is not inherently good, nor is Earth (symbolizing the body and subconscious) inherently bad.

The initiatory journey invites us to embrace the darkness and navigate cycles of light and shadow. Through this cyclical exploration, we attune ourselves to the natural rhythms of day and night and the changing seasons. Descending into the Underworld allows us to reconnect with the earth and recall the events that severed our connection with our bodies and fragmented our minds.

When trauma occurs, the body typically reacts with one of four automatic responses to danger or stress: fight, flight, freeze, or fawn.

- **Fight**: Confronting the threat with aggression or assertiveness.
- **Flight**: Escaping the threat by either physically running away or creating emotional distance.
- **Freeze**: Becoming immobile or paralyzed when faced with the threat.
- **Fawn**: Attempting to please or appease others to avoid conflict, as a way to diffuse the situation.

Over years of counseling clients, we've observed that the four trauma responses can be seen as progressive levels of reaction: Initially, a person may try to fight back; if that's not possible, they attempt to flee; when both fighting and fleeing fail, they freeze; and finally, they may resort to fawning, trying to appease the oppressor in the hope of survival. These responses can also occur simultaneously, as the subconscious mind searches for any possible way to reduce suffering.

This is the remarkable adaptability of the subconscious, always finding potential strategies for survival. However, within these trauma responses, we often tend to disconnect from our bodies, retreating into our minds or even dissociating completely.

While this ancient involuntary biological response to trauma is understandable, true healing begins when we ground ourselves back down into our bodies and reunite with our essence Self.

The best methods for grounding a person after a trauma experience often involve using the five senses to focus on the present moment, such as deep breathing exercises; actively noticing sights, sounds, smells, textures, and tastes around you; holding a textured object; or focusing on physical sensations, such as the feeling of your feet on the ground; and depending on the situation, a calming voice and reassurance from a trusted person can also be helpful.

There are many wonderful somatic-based trauma healing methods to assist with coming back into the body, such as craniosacral therapy or Peter Levine's Somatic Experiencing™, as well as the Focusing techniques of Eugene Gendlin.

It's true that you shouldn't venture down into the Underworld with no idea what you're doing. Venturing into the Underworld without guidance can be perilous, leading to internal harm. Learning to navigate the depths of our psyche is a skill that requires cultivation. Regardless of other self-improvement efforts, failure to address and integrate the Shadow, as well as our ego and judgments of others, will inevitably impede our progress.

A prime example of this can be found by looking at various spiritual leaders who seemingly have everything figured out and then revelations about their misuse of power begin to surface. Attempting to bypass the Shadow only leads to its eventual eruption. Before assuming roles of leadership, we must first earn trust by earnestly addressing our own trauma wounds.

NORMA'S Reflection

As a therapist for many years, I have had numerous occasions to be present with clients in varying states of psychosis. In our modern culture, I observed that their dissociated delusional states often bring forth metaphors of ascending up and out to the Upper World, where they identify with being a god, Christ, or a superhero, yet, they are unable to find the ancient pathway down into the earth, into the place where the Great Mother is holding their pain. This is fascinating, because it belies a long-standing cultural trauma, in which our minds flee to the Upper World and automatically seek "spiritual bypass."

We must address these compounded cultural trauma wounds so we can feel comfortable journeying down into the Underworld. Embedded in the collective unconscious, fear of the Underworld has made us reject the journey into the darkness and the pain held in the body. Much of Western medicine has been oriented toward numbing the symptoms of the pain. Although when the pain is too great it is important to give it relief, we have taken it a step too far by numbing beyond necessity. It is only by feeling enough, listening to the pain, and going skillfully into the unconscious realms that authentic healing can take place.

19

Navigating through a Drumming Journey

Successfully getting into and safely returning from the Underworld during a drumming journey requires the guidance of a map, as drumming journeys follow a specific pattern, a way to carefully go down into the earth of the Underworld and come back up again.

In this way, it is different from guided meditation. When someone else is guiding you, they are, in some ways, determining the course of your journey. However, with this way of doing a drumming journey, you are given the steps you must take in order to successfully enter an altered state and delve into the Underworld. From there, the direction your journey takes is unique to you.

As with any skill, journeying using drumming can take time to develop. It is normal for people to struggle in the beginning—struggle to let go, struggle to let their mind take them into the imaginal realms, struggle to feel like they are "doing it right." As you continue to work with your psyche in this way it will become easier.

You can find numerous recordings of steady drumming online to use as the drumbeat if you don't have someone in your immediate vicinity who can drum for you. Decide on the length of the drumming journey you would like to take, then find the appropriate recording. We recommend starting with 10–15 minutes of drumming.

To prepare for your drumming journey, set up your environment so that it is comfortable and undisturbed. Recline in a comfortable place with a pillow and blanket. Turn off your phone, close the door, and make sure you won't be interrupted during the entire process of the drum journey. It can also be helpful to be in a dimly lit room or cover your eyes with an eye mask. You don't want to fall asleep all the way; however, you want to be relaxed enough so that you can enter into a steady trance state. Once you have your drumming music picked out and your space set, you are ready to embark on your otherworldly adventure.

The following formula for the steps in the drum-induced trance journey, as Norma teaches it, has some unique elements you may not encounter elsewhere. Each of the stages in this process imparts important truths about how the altered-state terrain operates. There is an order to it, a natural set of laws. For example, just as the law of gravity determines what you can do in Ordinary Reality, guidelines should be followed as you navigate these other worlds.

Starting the Journey Properly to Assure a Safe Return

After you lie down to enter the drumming journey, you need to decide the following:

- Choose the portal entry place where you start your journey thoughtfully
- Choose the friend you will leave at the threshold and who will await your return

First, **select a place in Ordinary Reality** to imagine when you first close your eyes and the drumming begins. This place can be a spot from anywhere in your life you have actually visited. For example, some people like to start at the base of their favorite tree or a particular spot in their backyard from childhood.

Generally, this place is in the natural world rather than an urban environment, but what is most important is that it is somewhere that has significance for you. One person chose the long stairway down into the subway station where she walked each day. If you begin in a body of water, you must still go to the bottom and dig into the earth there. This exact place is where you will start your journey each time. It becomes your unique portal, or entry place.

Secondly, you need to decide who you are going to have waiting for you at the entry place. It's important to **leave a trusted friend at the portal of your journey**. This is not someone who is literally present in your physical environment but rather, a person or being you are calling upon to be there for you in the imaginal realms. It should be someone whom you trust and with whom you feel safe. They can be living or deceased; some people even pick a favorite pet. Leaving this being waiting for you signifies to your mind that you will return to this exact portal place and thereby, gives you a sense of security in taking off into the unknown, knowing that you will return to this familiarity.

You don't just do this once. With each journey, you always establish your portal place and the friend you are leaving there to wait for you. Only when these two initial choices are established does the drumming begin. You typically have the same entry place and person waiting or you for multiple drumming journeys. The time to choose different ones can occur after you have completed an entire round of one theme of your Shadow integration work over a significant period of time.

The Process for Going into the Underworld

Now that you have your portal entry point, lie down, close your eyes, and start the drumming journey. Study the surroundings in this place in your imagination that you have selected as your starting environment. Try to sensorially involve yourself in this familiar environment.

Survey the world you are seeing in your mind's eye. For example, do you see trees, grass, a stream? What is the color of the sky or the land? What do you hear? Birds chirping, creek water trickling? Imagine that you reach down and touch the earth. How does this particular dirt feel in your fingers? Bring it up to your nostrils to smell it. By involving your senses, you are drawing yourself further into the trance state and becoming immersed in this world in your mind's eye. Through engaging with your senses, you are also drawing your awareness away from your physical body, which is resting in Ordinary Reality. Now imagine saying goodbye to the friend you are leaving to wait for you while you go on this journey. Take comfort in the fact that you have a loved one who will be right there waiting for you while you go down into the depths of your psyche.

You make the transition from your physical reality into another state of consciousness every night when you go to sleep, so this process should not be entirely unfamiliar to you. However, this isn't about falling asleep and losing conscious awareness. You will still have some sense of your physical body that is lying down while also becoming immersed in this other reality. In some ways, it is a splitting of your awareness between the two worlds simultaneously. This is the pathway of the shamanic practitioner: to keep a foot in both worlds at once.

Now that you have become present in this new state of consciousness, your first task is to dig. **Put your mind to work digging into the earth**. This is the sole task to focus on. The mind loves to wander and become distracted. Giving it the task of digging is similar to focusing on your breath in other mindfulness practices that harness the "monkey mind" into presence with simple ways of keeping it focused.

You are digging down into the earth from that place with which you are so familiar. If that starting place happens to be a body of water, you must still go to the bottom and dig into the earth. So jump into the water, swim down until you reach the muddy bottom, and start digging there.

No matter where you start your journey, you must touch the earth and really feel the sensations of digging in it. If it is hard, solid ground, you can enlist the help of tools like a shovel, pick ax, and so on. But no matter what happens, just keep digging. The mind will want to wander. You may start thinking about what you are having for dinner or what you did at work. Whenever this happens, just refocus your intention on the task of digging. Going into the Underworld requires going into the earth, and digging is how you get there.

Eventually, you will reach a point where you make it all the way through to the other side. **The Underworld place can look different for each person**, even for each journey. Sometimes you will reach a cave; other times an open meadow or even your childhood home. It can often be surprising where you wind up.

At this point you aren't "just imagining" what will happen; you have broken into another state of consciousness, much like dreaming, where the experiences you are having are not just created by your conscious mind. In this space, things will surprise you. Be careful not to talk yourself out of the experience by thinking, *Oh, this isn't real, I'm just imagining it* or *I'm not doing this right; it should look this other way.* Trust the process, trust yourself, trust your psyche.

After you reach the other side of your digging, don't start wandering around. **First, you must find your power animal**, the one who will guide you in the Underworld. This point is really important and worth repeating: *Don't go any further in this space until you meet your power animal.*

Finding Your Power Animal in the Underworld

Your power animal is your guide for the Underworld within drumming journeys. You must follow your power animal wherever it goes, and you will be amazed to discover that it will lead you exactly where you need to go. Putting your trust in the power animal to guide you is what allows you to stay safe and balanced within the Underworld. It ensures that you do not venture into places in your psyche you are not ready to go to, and do not encounter experiences you are not ready for.

Throughout history, animals have been allies to humans. In many European, Asian, and Indigenous cultures, family lineage was identified by an animal clan. Wisdom traditions recognize the power of animals by wearing their skins and feathers and emulating their sounds and movements. Some researchers and anthropologists even believe that the emulation of animals is what originated human music and dance. Finding your particular power animal for this journey is about connecting to the inner guidance and earth-based wisdom of the animal realm.

Sitting or standing in the environment you've found yourself in, wait for the power animal to come to you. In the beginning, some people's journeys only get to this step. They just wait for the power animal and then are called back out of the journey before encountering one. That is okay. Wait as long as you need to, and don't become impatient or discouraged. Eventually, a power animal *will* always appear, although you may have to go on several more journeys and receive the lessons of the delay. When it does appear, you give the animal the Test of Four to ensure that it is really your power animal.

Identifying Your Power Animal through the Test of Four

The Test of Four means that you ask the power animal to show you four aspects of itself to make sure it is really your power animal.

For example, if an eagle comes flying over your head, and you ask it to do the Test of Four to prove it's your power animal, it may show you its eyes, talons, tail feathers, and wings. You have seen four different parts of it and therefore, know that it has appeared to you to become your power animal. If an elephant comes to you, it may show you its trunk, tail, feet, and large ears. Again, these are four different ways of perceiving it.

This step is so important, because you may find multiple animals visiting you in this Underworld space and become unsure which one to follow. Furthermore, sometimes an animal will come, and you feel uncertain about it. The Test of Four is a way to gain assurance that the animal you are meeting is meant for you.

Following Your Power Animal Ally

After this step of assurance, you are trusting and willing to follow your power animal into whatever experiences it guides you to within the trance state. They can be magical or mundane, simple or otherworldly. Your Ally may guide you to seeing past childhood experiences in new ways or transcendent experiences that bring you into contact with long-forgotten parts of yourself. It can be incredibly literal or symbolic. While on the journey it is not your job to interpret, just experience. Once you come back into Ordinary Reality you will have time to recount your journey and reflect on it. Try to set aside the rational mind while in this experience and immerse yourself in the unfolding as much as possible. Release the need to control and let yourself be guided.

After many journeying times together, you may get to the point of a test of your trust when the power animal will actually dismember or devour you. Don't be frightened if this happens. It is an indicator that it is time for ego deconstruction. By this point, you trust your spirit animal friend to "dismember" you in the symbolic realm, and ideally, your ego has been prepared by previous therapy and Dreamtime work so that you more easily allow the deconstruction.

The key understanding here is that this deconstruction can be safely experienced in the symbolic realm. As you'll recall, the unconscious is satisfied with the symbolic realm. In the Dreamtime, things can be experienced without physical pain or the same level of fear you have in ordinary consciousness. It is valuable to examine these fears and difficult realizations in the symbolic state of the journey, thereby preventing the Shadow from having to be lived out in Ordinary Reality, where physical form can be damaged.

Returning to Ordinary Reality

Find a drumming track that has a clear indication of when the drumming will be coming to an end. This often sounds like four drum beats close together a number of times, a pause, and then the drumbeat increasing in speed. The reason that this type of call back beat of the drum is important is that you need to know when it is getting close to ending so that you do not have to think about the end point and get preoccupied with that worry.

While the drum is beating at a more rapid pace, you enter the final stage of the drumming journey. It is important to **retrace every step of the journey in its entirety**. You want to go all the way back exactly the way you came. You can think of it like a film rewinding; visualize everything you just experienced being rewound in fast motion. Don't skip anything. It's important to collect each step and moment through this recollection.

In this step you are not only strengthening your memory of the journey, you are also strengthening the neural pathways in the brain you have just created in your inner perceptual process. In this way, the pathway will be more available and develop rapidly each time you return to the drum journey experience.

As the drum beats rapidly, make sure to go all the way back up the hole you dug on the way down, then find the friend you left at the threshold of the journey. Greet them and thank them for awaiting your return. This seals the container. At this point, the drumming will have stopped, and you can slowly bring your awareness back into the room, remembering all that you experienced in the Underworld.

20

Drumming Journey Examples

We will now give a few examples of drumming journeys that clients have permitted us to share. This will help ground the concepts of the pattern of a drumming journey. However, each person's drumming journey is extremely unique to them, and these examples are not intended to show you how your journey should look. Instead, they help you to see how the different elements of the pattern can happen for particular people, from digging down into the earth to finding one's power animal.

CLIENT EXAMPLE 1
Finding the Bear and Healing the Inner Child

I choose to leave Norma, my dear teacher, at the opening, where she will wait for me. I walk a little further past my familiar cabin, over to the corner of the pump house, where there is a hole in the ground.

I dig into the wet, muddy earth, imagining digging with my hands. I dig all the way through to the hot white sands of the San Joaquin Valley, where I spent my childhood, and then into the thick, sticky, orange-red Indian clay of Marin County, where I moved in my teen years.

My tunnel opens into a half-pipe. I slide down it as if I were on a waterslide. It veers sharply to the right, and I go careening down a slippery, very narrow passage, eventually landing on a hard brick surface. There is a circle of bricks all around me, and I realize that I have landed in a well.

I hear something unidentifiable. I look up to see a huge bear is falling down the long well shaft, head first. Making sure he is my power animal, I perform the Test of Four as he's falling. First,

I notice his open mouth and teeth, next his warm fur, then his paws, and finally his dark black eyes. Knowing that he is my power animal, I trust that he will guide me. He opens his mouth as he comes toward me and swallows me just as he lands.

I am surprised by this action but not afraid. I find myself just relaxed and doing a U-turn in his body, and as I do, now I am one with him, seeing through his eyes. We stretch our arms way, way, way up to the top of the well and pull ourselves up and out of the well.

Then to my amazement, the well fills up with firewood. When there is a huge pile from the bottom of the well to about 3 feet higher than the ground, we sit down on the logs of this pile. The logs then burst into flames, into a huge bonfire. We feel warm and toasty, not burnt at all, as can only happen in the Dreamtime.

Suddenly I see a baby version of myself crawling up to us. We hold and rock baby me for a while, then look up and see a kind woman walking up to us. She feels like a powerful otherworldly ally. We hand over the baby version of myself to her, and she pours various colors of light onto me. Like a rainbow of love, it feels profoundly healing.

Eventually, I hear the drumbeat beckoning me back into Ordinary Reality, so I go backward through the process. I emerge from the earth and greet Norma, who is waiting there for me.

For this next drumming journey, the Intent of the voyager was to release the anger toward his abusive father he was holding onto.

CLIENT EXAMPLE 2
Flying with the Eagle to the Childhood Home to Face Past Wounds

I left my dear friend at my portal into the Underworld. I was already upset but determined to heal this anger I was feeling.

I started digging and was able to drop down into the hole quickly. I've been doing drumming journeys for a while at this point, so I already have the power animal of the eagle. My eagle came to me, and I can see to the other side of the hole I'm digging that there is a blue sky.

Dropping down through the hole, I become one with the eagle and fly to the other side, and to my surprise I land on my own shoulder.

I see a big statue of the family member I'm so upset with. The statue is somewhat alive, and when I get close to it, the statue tries to grab me. However, I know that I have power in this situation, and it's not able to reach me. One of my adult children comes to me as a two-year-old and tells me I need to protect them; I know that I can.

The statue begins to crumble, and as it does, I feel my anger fading away. My eagle picks me up on its back, and we fly down into a darker and darker place, going deeper in, and then my childhood home appears. I must face the ghosts of my past in this childhood home. It brings me to tears, and my eagle comforts me. I'm able to surround everyone I love in a beautiful blue sphere and send them to a safe area away from my childhood home.

My eagle picks me up and we fly high and then around the world. I see how there are a lot of hard things that people have to go through on this planet, and I feel the grief of that. With my eagle by my side in this state, I'm able to hold great compassion and feel fearless. I know that I can't be harmed in this state, and I can be a force for good and light.

I hear the call to come back to Ordinary Reality and feel a profound shift within me. I retrace my steps and return to my friend, who I left waiting there for me at the portal.

The power animal that comes to you represents an energy that wants to become more integrated within you. This next client found out just how true this is when he first met his power animal.

CLIENT EXAMPLE 3
Finding the Fox Power Animal and the Joy of Play

I decide to dig down in my front yard, near my favorite tree. I leave my wife there waiting for me and begin digging in the earth. At a certain point, I get stuck digging, then I realize that I can conjure something to help me, using my imagination. I summon a digging crane machine and use that to dig my hole more easily.

Finally, I make it all the way through and arrive in a dark cave. Looking around I see this animal darting through the darkness. I can only catch a flash of it before it disappears. Next, the animal runs right up to me and stops in front of my face. It's a fox! As quickly as it comes up, it leaps away.

The fox is bouncing from one thing to the next. It comes up behind me and jumps on my back. It goes away again, then comes on my side and takes a hold of my right hand to dance with me. After that, the fox comes up on my left side and invites me to jump with him and roll and play. With that, the fox had shown up in four different ways and so I know it is my power animal because it completed the Test of Four.

It is so playful and delightful. My Shadow work right now is all about not having enough fun in my life. I feel like I'm all work and no play, so having this power animal and the playful energy it presents is perfect for me. I'm so happy to be connected with the fox as my animal guide.

21

Integrating a Drumming Journey

It is very important to take time to integrate any altered-state experience upon your return. Currently, with the popularity of psychedelic journeys, there is a lot of discussion about the right ways to integrate afterwards. Drumming journeys are not as intense as most psychedelic adventures, but they too need time for you to learn from the lessons you gleaned in the liminal realms.

Upon returning to Ordinary Reality from a drumming journey, slowly start to wiggle your toes and bring yourself back into your body. Take some deep breaths, and gently open your eyes. Now is the time to capture the story of what just happened to you. If you are with other people, each person should take a turn sharing their journey with the group.

Unless you are with a guide certified in the Journey to Completion or someone expert in drumming journeys and human psychology, it is best to refrain from having other people interpret your journey. Instead, the mere act of speaking it out loud to the group will often bring about your own profound revelations. Much like sharing a dream once you've woken up, telling your story helps unlock the symbolic messages within the journey.

Speaking your journey aloud helps ground your experience in your Ordinary Reality; that is, it anchors your experience back in your everyday life, where the gifts from the drumming journey can bear fruit. Even if you don't have someone to whom you can speak about your journey immediately, find a trusted companion, friend, or therapist to share it with over the following hours or days.

In addition, always make sure that you write down your journey. Since you retraced your steps through the whole journey, you should be able to remember everything that happened. Write it out in as much detail as possible, so that when you revisit your writing you can reenter the liminal experience of your trance-state journey. Drawing the journey, even if you use stick figures, is another way to remember and unlock its symbolic meaning.

Meeting your power animal within the journey is a profound gift for your life, not just for the moment. Throughout the entire round of the Journey to Completion process you have the same power animal. The relationship with a particular animal presence becomes very loving and personal as you go on multiple drum journeys and learn to trust its guidance over time. People can have many different power animals throughout their lifetime if they are regularly doing this work, and each one offers a unique set of qualities that you currently need in your life.

Reflect on the Following Questions in Your Journal

Take the time to think of the power animal that came to meet and guide you:

- What did it feel like to be in its presence?
- How did it move, how did it interact with you?
- What was its personality?
- Write a list of energetic qualities that it shares with you.

The energetic configurations of the power animal offer you lessons for your own life.

For example, from a bear you might feel the need for more rest and to learn how to balance being active and hibernating, while a hawk may hold the lesson of staying focused on exactly what you want and then striking at just the right moment to get it.

After you've had a chance to do your own reflection, you can go online and look up what others have written about specific power animals and their qualities. Oftentimes, you will be shocked by the synchronicities in what is written and what is currently going on in your life.

It's no coincidence which power animal comes to you. Transcribe in your journal the key points you learn about your power animal from your online searches. There is a plethora of information out there about power animals, and each one is someone's interpretation, so take time to look at a few different write-ups and take from them what resonates with you the most.

Power animals will often come to you in Ordinary Reality once you've encountered them in the drumming journeys. Many students have been shocked to see how their power animal appears to them in their lives. If your power animal is a more commonly encountered animal, such as a squirrel, you might start seeing squirrels crossing your path every time you go down your driveway or have one stop and stare at you for extended periods of time and even follow along as you are walking. If your power animal is one you normally wouldn't encounter in your daily life, such as a black panther, you may experience a friend giving you a birthday card with a panther on it, unaware that it is your power animal.

As you do more and more drumming journeys, you will start to develop the muscle of venturing into the Underworld and retrieving the lessons held there. Through writing down each experience, you begin to catalog the terrain of your inner world. You will start to notice synchronicities, recurring issues, and themes come through. This is the work of your own map-making. You are learning to navigate your unconscious mind and make meaning out of the messages it is presenting you with. The more journeys you do, the more profound and clear the messages will become.

Why Drumming Journeys Are an Important Step in Navigating Your Psyche

In building the ability to go into a trance state through drumming journeys, you are preparing yourself to know how to cross between Ordinary Reality and the Dreamtime without losing consciousness.

This ability is a key skill to unlock for successful lucid dreaming. Furthermore, if you do psychedelics, you will know how to maintain a thread of lucidity as you cross from Ordinary Reality into the liminal. You will also more deeply understand the symbols that are coming to you through the plant medicine-induced hallucinations.

We always tell people that you don't need to do plant medicines to do the Journey to Completion training and drumming journeys, but you *should* do the Journey to Completion and drumming journeys to understand how to navigate plant medicine skillfully. Drumming journeys are honing your skill set to be able to steer the ship of your awareness through the uncharted waters of the unconscious and Dreamtime.

When you ingest a psychedelic, you are bringing the Dreamtime into Ordinary Reality. However, the consequences of Ordinary Reality still exist, because that is where you are. If, for example, you are on a psychedelic trip and become frantic, leave your safe space, and get in trouble for acting out, you will come back into non-altered consciousness realizing that you have to deal with the waking reality consequences of your actions.

During a drumming journey, you can safely explore and work through fearful experiences without real-world consequences. As you navigate these altered states of consciousness, you learn to stay grounded even when encountering phenomena that don't exist in Ordinary Reality. This practice builds your ability to maintain lucidity and composure while experiencing non-ordinary states of consciousness.

PART 3

Dreaming

22

What Is Lucid Dreaming?

When you go to sleep each night, you have the potential to "wake up." In the case of psychonavigation, the ability to become lucid within your dream presents a profound opportunity to work with your psyche directly, coming face to face with the hidden parts of yourself.

Imagine being able to have a conversation with your inner child and to be able to ask them what hurt them in the past or facing the "boogeyman" in your dream only to discover it was an aspect of your own personality you were demonizing. All of this is possible once you unlock the skill of lucidity.

As Tenzin Wangyal Rinpoche says in *The Tibetan Yogas of Dream and Sleep*, when we wake in the morning and continue in "real" life, as if we are still asleep and dreaming, then we will continue to be in this deluded, dreamy state, day and night.

As illustrated in the quote above, most of us are not fully awake even when in waking reality. We travel habitually round and round between old beliefs, fantasies about the future, and regrets about the past. The present moment remains unnoticed and unrecognized for the exceptional gift of lucidity it holds. The practice of working with the Dreamtime and striving for lucidity is one of becoming present in every moment. It is possible to wake up to the truth of what is meant by "living in continual presence."

Before elucidating the full scope of what is possible within lucid dreaming, it is helpful to have a clear definition of what lucid dreaming is. A lucid dream is a dream in which you are completely aware that you are dreaming during the dream.

Most people have had at least one experience of lucid dreaming in their lives. It can spontaneously happen—you are in a dream and then have an "aha" moment of waking up to the fact that you are dreaming.

Sometimes, the realization can come from a nightmare in which you realize you are dreaming and forcefully wake yourself up, or through an unusual situation within your dream that is too uncanny to ignore.

Many people report that in childhood they had spontaneous lucid dreams somewhat regularly. Spontaneous lucid dreams are a great indicator that the psyche is primed to have the realization of dreaming within the dream. However, if this hasn't been the case for you, don't be discouraged. Lucid dreaming is a skill that can be developed. As with any other talent, with enough dedication and practice it can be honed, and regular lucid dreaming will become possible.

At any stage of lucid dreaming a clear and precise Intent is a key ingredient. The Intent is what propels you forward to growing your lucid dreaming abilities through each stage. The progression of your Intent while lucid dreaming could allow you:

- To become lucid
- To sustain the lucid state for longer periods of time
- To enjoy the pleasures of lucid dreaming
- To face fears within the lucid state
- To connect with guides and your higher self

All of these steps are ways of working with and understanding your psyche. It should also be noted that there are different levels of lucidity within lucid dreaming. Some people mistake a beginning level for full lucidity. If you've had a slight inclination that you could be dreaming within the dream but continue as usual, without complete recognition of the reality that you are dreaming, that is not full lucidity. Similarly, waking up after a dream and thinking, *Oh, I kind of knew it was a dream,* is also not full lucidity.

Signs that it was *not* a fully lucid dream are:

- Slightly knowing you were dreaming but having no power to affect the dream

- A moment of thinking it was a dream but then slipping back into the dream material without retaining that realization

Full Lucidity Comes When You Know that You Are Dreaming while Still Asleep

When full lucidity "clicks on," the dream takes on a different quality. The dream is no longer hazy, and all of your senses come online as much as they are in waking reality. Everything feels very visceral, and you can smell, taste, and touch things just as you would while awake. In fact, it feels as real as being awake—sometimes, it might even feel *more* real than waking reality. If you've had a fully lucid dream in your life, chances are you know it beyond a doubt, because it is such a unique and enlivening experience.

Tenzin Wangyal Rinpoche states, "With experience, greater freedom is developed in the dream and the boundaries of the mind are overcome, until one can do literally anything that one can think of to do."

In a lucid state, you can marvel at all that the mind is capable of creating. From this, there is a direct experiential realization of how much the mind is responsible for creating reality.

Some people worry that when experiencing the realness of lucid dreaming, they may begin to get confused about the differences between waking reality and the Dreamtime. Although this is unlikely for most people, it is a great reason to dedicate oneself to the skill of psychonavigation. Learning to live with polyphasic awareness means being conscious of what phase of reality you are in at any particular moment and the distinct qualities of each dimension of perception.

There are rules and limitations within the various realms of consciousness, and learning those rules is not only helpful but also essential the more advanced you become. Obviously, if you win the lottery in a dream, you will not wake up with a bank account full of money. Just because you can fly within a lucid dream does not mean you should try to fly off a balcony while awake.

Respecting the rules of Ordinary Reality keeps you safe and alive. On some occasions when people take psychedelics, they lose track of what reality they are in and forget its rules. This can lead to dire consequences that carry on beyond the trip. Although these are extreme cases, by strengthening the muscles of an observant mind you better prepare yourself to avoid making mistakes when in highly altered states, or when applying the lessons after you come back into Ordinary Reality.

Drumming journeys, lucid dreams, out-of-body experiences, psychedelic journeys, and Ordinary Reality all have rules. Study them, learn them, as this is a key component to psychonavigating.

Examples of Some of the Rules in the Different Realities

- **In waking reality**, we know that there is cause and effect, linear time, and Newtonian physics. One action follows the next, gravity pulls us down when we jump up, and when our bodies are hurt or broken, they take time to heal.
- **In drumming journeys**, you need to notice the physical setting first, as the guidance takes place within the particular physical environment. That is why it is so important to start the journeys in a known, "real world," imagined environment and then go from there. The environments are your anchors into realization.
- **In lucid dreams**, gravity is more malleable, and flying is possible, you can shift environments from one space to another, and creating portals like doors and mirrors is a great way to travel between dream spaces.
- **In out-of-body experiences**, things can be a little more solid than lucid dreams. For example, it can be harder to go through walls.

These are just a few examples, and these rules come from our own first-hand experiences and work with clients. Since many of these realms are constructed in your psyche, it's also important to learn what your personal rules are as they may be slightly different. Find and note them for yourself.

Although you cannot carry over accomplishments like winning the lottery into waking reality from a lucid dream, psychological accomplishments do very much carry over. When you can work through a reoccurring fear or limiting belief in your dream, you can wake up with a psychological shift effective in Ordinary Reality.

The unhealed ego can often take on a know-it-all superiority and claim dominance over others after returning from an altered-state experience; therefore, one of the first rules in these realms is to surrender and turn over the ego pride in a humble taking on of self-responsibility for any Shadow projections.

You may feel extreme pain at what you have endured at the hands of others, but even so, the goal of healing in the trance states is a non-dualistic outcome. You may need to express anger and rage in the altered-state realms, but the journey through your emotions will eventually lead to the healing of the wound. This change in perspective will lead to a new kind of empowerment. Seeing with new eyes, you will be able to view situations from a place of union that is non-dualistic not blaming, and one with all that is.

Working on energetic difficulties and limitations of the mind within your dream produces a flexibility of mind that is one of the key goals within many wisdom traditions, including Tibetan Dream Yoga. A flexible mind is one that overcomes the limitations of "wrong views" that constrict experience and keep us trapped in habitual cycles of behavior. As long as one is trapped inside a rigid mind, true freedom will never be available, but when the mind is flexible we can overcome grasping and aversion, because we see things in a new way rather than being driven by ingrained reactions.

Ultimately, true freedom comes from liberating the psyche from its stuck places. It is not necessarily something you arrive at and then have for the rest of your life; rather, continually assessing and freeing up the rigid places of the mind is the practice of a lifetime. Having the tools to enter trance states, become lucid in dreams, use psychedelics at key moments, and constantly do your Shadow work help keep the mind flexible and adaptable. Moving into this way of living creates a reality—whether asleep or awake—that is more comfortable, clear, easy, and integrated.

In Dream Yoga, the purpose of training one's mind to operate in this way is liberation within the *bardo* states after death. In the Buddhist tradition, it is believed that after you die you enter the liminal states of the bardo. In simplified terms, in these bardo states, you can become distracted and distraught by the illusions your mind creates, just as you would within a dream. If you have not trained the mind to recognize these manifestations of the mind as illusory (as they are in a dream), you will fearfully run into a karmic rebirth or get stuck in various mental/emotional reactionary realms.

Tenzin Wangyal Rinpoche said:

"The Mother Tantra says that if one is not aware in vision, it is unlikely that one will be aware in behavior. If one is not aware in behavior, one is unlikely to be aware in dream. And if one is not aware in dream, then one is unlikely to be aware in the bardo after death."

Whether the Buddhist view of what happens after death resonates with you or not, cultivating a mind that is aware during this lifetime prepares you to work with the bardos (liminal moments of change) within this lifetime. That is valuable in itself, as the bardos can also be viewed as experiences not limited to the after-death state but rather, mental and emotional states where we all can become stuck during life. We have all experienced rage, envy, longing, jealousy, ignorance, and pride in our lives. In the course of a single day, you might move through many of these "bardo realms" of emotion.

Recognizing these states as actual realms where you can get stuck is a helpful practice for seeing the ruts in your psyche. If you find yourself constantly angry, or encountering and dealing with people who are always angry with you, recognizing this as a "resonant reality" (a familiar realm you visit) can be the first step to becoming lucid. This recognition can show you what you should focus on healing.

Similarly, if you are having dreams that are constantly violent and filled with rage, this is a good indicator that your psyche is crying out for you to pay attention to some hurt you have buried in your subconscious. As you develop a "continuity of awareness" (the ability to notice what is revealing itself to you in your life and dreams), you can take hold of the Shadow material presenting itself. Study the material and write down challenging experiences you are having while awake and asleep. See if there is a Shadow wound theme emerging.

The gift of the Dreamtime is beckoning you, like a treasure chest filled with insight. Will you answer the Call?

23

The Dreamer as Shaman

> *Sorcerers view dreaming as an extremely sophisticated art...*
> *the art of of displacing the assemblage point at will from its*
> *habitual position in order to enhance and enlarge the scope*
> *of what can be perceived.*
> —CARLOS CASTANEDA, The Art of Dreaming

In *The Art of Dreaming*, Carlos Castaneda writes at length about how the Nagual sorcerers framed the fact that when you are dreaming, perception is naturally brought into an altered state. Through the framework of his lineage, Castaneda claims that the "assemblage point" in a person is what determines the version of reality they are experiencing. As discussed previously, the assemblage point can be viewed by those with "second sight" as collected filaments of light inside a luminous egg-shaped ball that exists around all people.

The Nagual goal of developing what they call "second attention" is similar to the concept of "second sight" explored in the Celtic lineage.

For the Nagual, "first attention" represents the awareness of our daily world, which we perceive through our habitual assemblage point while we are awake. To develop second attention, we must move the assemblage point to other spaces in order to perceive other worlds that are different from Ordinary Reality. Castaneda explains his experience of reaching the second attention as a "disturbing state of unequaled clarity or superconsciousness." It is similar to a strange or lucid dream.

Displacing the assemblage point was one of the main tasks and goals of the sorcerers. Don Juan explains that the sorcerers devised extravagant techniques to displace the assemblage point, such as ingesting psychoactive plants, fasting, and extreme physical exertion.

They also discovered that when we sleep, the assemblage point can very easily be displaced. In fact, dreams are actually the result of a displaced assemblage point. The more displaced the assemblage point becomes, the more unusual the dream. Thus, the sorcerers went to work controlling their dreams (lucid dreaming) in order to move the assemblage point dramatically and thus, view realities entirely different from our own.

Alongside displacement of the assemblage point, one must also dedicate oneself to total recall. Castaneda writes at length about how sorcerers would dedicate themselves to the task of remembering everything experienced while in the "second attention" (dream realms). Remembering the experiences you had within lucid dreams, and recording them, ensures that you retain the power received from them and integrate the lessons into your waking reality.

Castaneda elucidates a key point—that the mind can be altered just as much by dreaming as it can by the ingestion of psychedelics. What's more, dreaming is something that takes place naturally every night without the need for any external stimuli.

To harness the power of lucid dreaming is to become a "sorcerer" of consciousness. The assemblage point can be moved to various nonordinary states of awareness through dreaming, from the relatively mundane to the transcendental. Through discipline and dedication, the sorcerer succeeds in displacing the assemblage point more and more drastically to produce transformational experiences.

One of our beloved teachers, a Brazilian healer named Tate Angela, once said, "Anyone who pays attention to her dreams is being a little shaman." A shaman is someone whose life work in the tribe is dedicated to bringing healing to others. The first step to bring healing to our tribe is to wake up, recall, and share your dreams around the breakfast table.

When you cross the threshold from Ordinary Reality into the Dreamtime you are venturing into a space where tremendous insight can be gleaned. Most people have had the experience at some point in their lives of going to bed with a problem on their minds and waking up with the solution. Similarly, when you diligently write down your dreams and look back on them, you may come to recognize how they held premonitions for what was to come. Shamans not only dreamed for themselves but also for others in their communities. People would come with their problems and then the shaman would go to sleep, into the Dreamtime, to find solutions.

NORMA'S Childhood of Dreaming

Where I grew up, near the Seneca, Iroquois territory, we were taken to the ritual circles, where we saw strange masks of faces on high poles. We were told that the faces represented Dreamtime beings that were an important part of our lives, just as important as living human beings.

This reflects the Iroquois concept of *katera'swas*. The English translation of this word is "I dream," but as with many words, there can be much lost in translation. *Katera'swas* means so much more than when we say the phrase "I dream" in English. *Katera'swas* means, "You must have dreaming as a habit, as a daily part of your way of being in the world." The expression also carries the connotation of manifestation, as in, "I bring myself luck because I can bring about good fortune or prosperity through my dreaming." In fact, Iroquois elders taught us that we would have bad luck if we ignored our dreams.

Along with being wounded healers, walkers between the worlds, and negotiators with spirits, the predominant characteristic of all shamans is that they are strong dreamers.

The first calling onto the shamanic path is typically received in one's dreams. Shamans are also initiated and trained in their Dreamtime. That is what happened to me. I started having strong dreams when I was very young—dreams of being visited by kind, loving animals, of being taken into space and shown wonders beyond my ability to almost describe.

By the time I was seven, my grandmother and the elders told my parents that I had the Calling. From a young age, I was met in my dreams by guides (power animals). The golden eagle and the horse came to me as loving allies. I was taken to many beautiful experiences of earthly gardens and cosmic dimensions, and I was also taken through many ordeals in the Dreamtime.

As you've learned about drumming journeys, one must find one's animal guides and then venture into the Underworld (challenges and traumas), the Upper World (cosmic dimensions), and the Middle World (this time/space reality). At that young age, I didn't comprehend that my dreams were taking me through the various worlds the shaman perpetually traverses and teaching me how to walk that path, but looking back on it I am amazed.

I was taught to be brave and not run from the devouring bears and cauldrons of boiling water. I came to understand that the Dreamtime was a symbolic realm where I could experiment with remembering and facing my fears. I was taught to trust deeply that all was working together for my good, and that I was being guided by powers greater than myself for my learning.

Dreams remind us of our soul's greater calling in this life. When we stray off the path, sometimes a shocking dream is the only thing that can wake us from the stupor of complacency and get us back on track.

One time, I dreamed that I was carrying a suitcase filled with many shoes, but no shoes matched. Later that week, I was led to a book where I discovered the meaning of the dream. Celtic shamans were often called "one-shoed" or "one-footed" because they lived part-time in this world and part-time in the other—one foot in each world so to speak.

This was a timely discovery, which gave me the courage to pursue the next level of my psychonavigation adventure. I knew that I had a Calling to walk between the worlds with one foot firmly planted in Ordinary Reality and the other in the liminal realms of the Dreamtime. Since you are reading this book chances are that you also have heard the Calling!

Perhaps you have had similar experiences in your dreams—ones where you were walking through these worlds and learning lessons as you did so. It is a shame that in our culture we are not trained to be on the lookout for what worlds we are walking in during our sleep. Understanding more fully the landscapes we navigate while asleep is the essential tool for integrating the lessons of our dreams into our waking reality.

Humans have often wondered what the purpose of dreaming is. However, there isn't just one type of dreaming; there are many kinds of dreams: big dreams, little dreams, dreams for self, dreams for others, prophetic dreams, and dreams that must be acted out or we will not be able to progress in Ordinary Reality.

Let us take our dreams seriously and act upon them. The reservoir of the mind is indeed vast. Through dreamwork, we create an awareness of the fact that we have access to much more information than is apparent from how we usually operate in Ordinary Reality. By harnessing the depths of our subconscious mind lucidly, we can harness the innate problem-solving function of our sleeping mind. But the Dreamtime will bear no fruit if we don't pay attention to it. We must choose to remember and act upon the messages of our dreams.

We must wake up in our dreams and apply this wisdom so desperately needed now. The Hindu teaching says we are at the end of the Kali-yuga. We must continue, unafraid of being on the verge of something tremendously new. Great lucidity is necessary for humanity to navigate these times successfully.

In the book *Black Elk Speaks*, it is revealed that shamans have four great dreams in their lifetime. These dreams lay the template for the events that will unfold in their times. The four dreams are recognized as unique because they all start in the same way and contain an unfolding prophetic message.

NORMA'S Four Prophetic Dreams

Before I read the book *Black Elk Speaks*, I had these four dreams. When I did finally read the book, it confirmed for me that my dreams were the kind of special dream that a shaman is given for the benefit of their people.

I was given the four prophetic dreams throughout my 20s into my late 30s. I knew these particular dreams were important and that they were related, because they each began with the same very unusual imagery. Each dream is built on the last one, with significant information revealed at each step.

This information may now sound more acceptable and palatable, but in the years when I had these dreams (1970s–1980s), no one was speaking of such things. These dreams came before the obsession with the end of time in 2012, before the back to land and permaculture movements, and well before it was acceptable to speak of alien spaceships.

Each dream began in the following way:

I was with a group of familiar people, like a tribal community, and we were all outside looking up into the sky at a very shocking, bizarre, never-before-witnessed phenomenon: There were two suns visible in the sky. Then we saw a huge round clock burst apart and heard a loud voice speak, "You shall be living through the end of time as you know it!" Then what followed in each dream built upon the previous one.

FIRST DREAM: I was in a light blue-colored Volkswagen, and suddenly it was swept up in a whirlwind and blown through a wormhole tunnel in time/space and landed in an ancient time. All around me, dust was flying, as humans were rushing about in a panic. There were horse-drawn carts loaded with all their belongings and cries of fear and anguish as these people were fleeing. A voice spoke to me, saying, "Observe this well, because you too will be living through the end of civilization as you know it."

SECOND DREAM: We now had come to be living in a community with this same tribe of people. We were being instructed to build round structures and plant gardens and dwell in sustainable harmony in the countryside. It was as if the veils had fallen from our eyes and we were each fully awakened to our creative proclivity and task. We were operating in a smooth flow together, each one fulfilled and productive in meaningful work. My role was being part of a group of healers, martial artists, and dancers who went from town to town, reminding people of the ancient, embodied practices of Shadow work, so that the communities could live in harmony and productivity and not be divided by division and fighting.

THIRD DREAM: Again, in this same community of now long-time trusted allies, we were given the message that one element was still needed to complete our communal configuration for its full potency, and what we needed was more men who were "Ramakrishnas." When I had this dream in my early 30s, I had never heard the term "Ramakrishna," because at that time I hadn't studied Hindu culture. Later I was surprised to read that Ramakrishna was a man who was the primary devotee of the goddess Kali.

After that dream, I studied deeply the life and teachings of Ramakrishna and the meaning of the deity of Kali. I even took a three-year initiatory training to become a devotee of Kali. This goddess is symbolically very significant for our times because she is the dark goddess who brings the end of patriarchal domination and the return of feminine powers to Earth. The men who are like Ramakrishna are devoted to the feminine and spiritual evolution of the planet by the rebalancing of the masculine and feminine energies. A radical statement describing the power of Kali is that she will destroy whatever needs to be destroyed in order for the great harmony to return.

FOURTH DREAM: The whole community was together in a large, cathedral-type, round structure on the land. The building was on a brown dried-grass mountain side, and we were looking out of huge windows that overlooked a vast valley and a green mountain range. As we were watching the sky, two suns appeared and then we saw bursting into our visible reality a group of round spaceships. They came and landed in the field above our property, and the whole community rushed out to greet them.

Each of us seemed identified with particular friends aboard the spaceships. It was shown to us that we were part of a grid on Earth and these beings were our grid-mates from the heavens coming to reunite with each of us. My grid-mate was a short, plump, older man with white hair from India. When I saw him, I recognized him as an old dear friend, and we hugged and I wept tears of joy in being reunited.

Then I asked him, "Now that you have returned, is it going to be a scary time of Earth changes and cataclysmic destruction?"

He looked me right in the eye and his eyes were so loving and kind and he said, "No, not at all. We have come to remind you that things can all change in the twinkling of an eye. There is no need for fear."

Then I woke up and told my daughter the dream to this point. She said to me, "That was not the end of the dream, was it?"

She is a very psychically attuned being, and because she said this, I was then able to remember what happened next.

What happened next was so far beyond my capacity to understand that it had been difficult to even remember. A grid from the heavens came down and aligned with a grid on Earth, and a giant synching up happened that was like a reuniting of Heaven and Earth. I felt this sensation of being "at home" on Earth in a way I had never felt before. The sensation was one of floating, as if the law of gravity had been released. The feeling was of Heaven and Earth being reunited after a long separation.

That dream in particular has given me great confidence about what we are going through in these challenging times.

Think back through your own dreams; have you had a series like this? What have been the key dreams of your lifetime thus far?

24

Imbalance between the Dreamtime and Ordinary Reality

Connecting with your Dreamtime isn't about running away from the reality of mundane life—quite the opposite. Honoring the Dreamtime is about realizing the interconnectedness between the world of dreams and that of waking reality. One does not exist without the other.

The fact is that as we bring conscious lucid awareness into our dreams, we become more lucid in Ordinary Reality. Attaining a good balance between the realms of consciousness is the accomplishment of the adept psychonavigator.

In *The Tibetan Yogas of Dream and Sleep,* we are reminded: "Normally the dream is thought to be 'unreal,' as opposed to 'real' waking life. But there is nothing more real than a dream."

Our psyches have been split in two, and we have been made to believe that what we do while awake is all that matters and what we do while asleep should be forgotten. However, once you are able to integrate the Dreamtime and Ordinary Reality, you will find that you can bring together a fulcrum of power not available when fragmented between the two realities.

It could be said that the most recent surge in interest in psychedelics is an outcry from our current collective consciousness for a reconnection with the Dreamtime. This is because hallucinogenic substances bring the Dreamtime into Ordinary Reality and let us know that the mythical and magical can be experienced as real. The issue with only accessing the Dreamtime using psychedelics is that a dependence on an external source of mystical gnosis can develop.

Inside you is the ability to connect directly with profound and transformational experiences beyond the rational mind; furthermore, this state can be available to you each night when you go to sleep. It requires cultivating a relationship with your dreamworld and honoring it rather than diminishing its potency.

As you progress in your exploration of the Dreamtime, things will begin happening in your Ordinary Reality that were foretold in your dreams. Night and day start to sync up, and as this happens, it's a signal that you are really listening to your Dreamtime and a harmonization is happening between the two realms.

Dreams Prepare You for Navigating Change and Death

As you explore the realm of your dreams, you begin to recognize the narrative that underlies waking reality: a constant quest for survival, where every moment is spent anticipating the next threat and striving for control over every situation.

The Dreamtime can be unpredictable and ever-changing, but have you noticed a profound secret? Life itself is always in a state of flux, just like the Dreamtime. We often assume that stability and routine bring stasis and that things will remain the same if we can simply maintain control over our daily lives. But while waking reality may not unfold as dramatically as a dream, change is always lurking, waiting to disrupt the status quo.

It's during moments of flux that we're most acutely aware of the presence of change. One day, life can be humming along smoothly and then an unexpected event can throw us into a state of liminality. A job loss, a breakup, or a move to a new home or city can shatter our ordinary routine, forcing us to confront the reality of change head on. Whether the upheaval lasts for days, weeks, months, or years, change is an unwavering companion on our journey through life.

At its core, the fear of change often stems from the fear of the ultimate change that awaits us all: death. The prospect of mortality can be overwhelming when we consider that one day we'll have to surrender everything to a reality that's vastly different from our waking experience:

the great unknown. It's no wonder that even small changes in our daily lives can fill us with anxiety. By acknowledging and accepting this fear, we may find it easier to face the uncertainty that comes with every transition.

NISHA'S Story of Death Calling Her to the Dreamtime

The realization of death came to me in the most visceral way I have ever experienced when I was 26 years old.

It was a normal day, I was driving along in the car with my mom, and off the cuff, like I had done so many times before, I said, "Someday, when I die . . ."

However, unlike so many times before, when that phrase felt so far away, so inconceivable, this day it was fully present with all its weight and force. Those words, "Someday when I die . . . ," crashed down upon me and pushed my awareness out of the mundane into a parallel sensory dimension.

I felt death surrounding me, and there was nowhere to hide from it. The presence of death felt like a truly uncomfortable drug trip, where one moment I was in the car with my mom "chit-chatting" and casually bringing up death and the next moment I was being flung into the void itself. And boy, was I shaken!

I stopped talking, because I had no other words left in my mind—only the feeling that someday I was going to have to leave everything I knew and held so dearly in this reality and venture into the unknown. This moment was not a passing one. It stuck with me deeply for the whole year. I would wake up, anxiety-ridden, with the thought, "Oh my god, I'm going to die, and I don't know what will happen after that."

Before this moment I had never had existential panic, but afterwards it was a daily occurrence.

That mundane utterance in the car with my mom triggered a near-death experience in my consciousness. It wasn't so close that I saw angels and a light at the end of a tunnel; rather, it was the kind of "close" where you are trying to peek around a drawn curtain but can't see what lies behind.

You may be able to relate to this fear. Perhaps it didn't come rushing in all at once. Maybe, instead, it's just a subtle feeling in the back of your head, a whisper saying, "Someday you will die, and that's scary."

Before this moment, I always thought that I was at peace with death. As a child, I don't remember fearing it at all. I had this feeling that no matter whether I died or lived, everything was going to be fine. The same is true of my teenage years.

At the threshold of turning 26 years old, when I was leaving childhood behind and entering adulthood, I finally got what all the fuss was about. I felt the reality and permanence of death in full force.

However, I didn't stay in those depths of existential dread. I journeyed through the fears of death, into the unknown of the Dreamtime, and back out into freedom. This freedom comes through living, dreaming, and dying lucidly.

There are many ways to come face to face with death. It can happen when someone close to you dies, through personal illness, or after surviving a near-death experience. Chances are, most people have confronted their mortality at some point in their life, and not liked what they saw.

In my own case, my year of being consumed by the fear of death was the biggest gift to my life. Since I was faced with it relentlessly each day, I had no choice but to dive head first into finding a way to assuage it.

As I contemplated death, I was impacted by the fact that there exists this realm both unknown and unexplored by our waking minds – a foreign territory we all venture into each night: the Dreamtime. To understand what happens after we die, we are given the Dreamtime to explore now.

From the Tibetan Buddhist perspective, seeing how you work with the mind in dreams is an indicator of how you will navigate the bardos after you die. Since the liminal state of death is about navigating the illusions created by the mind, you can practice navigating those illusions while asleep. If your dreams are fearful, scattered, or unconscious, practice bringing lucidity into the dream space in preparation for death. When the messages of sleep are clear, and you are present within the Dreamtime, you become more fully awake in the various phases of consciousness.

The shamanic Calling often involves an encounter with death and a return to the body. This transformative and initiatory experience marks the shaman's path. The profound experience of a near-death experience can take various forms and symbolize the shaman's transition from Ordinary Reality to the spiritual realm.

Many people undergo a crisis that can be physical, emotional, or spiritual. Physically, it can manifest as a severe illness or accident. Emotionally, it might involve extreme states of depression, hopelessness, or fear. Spiritually, it can look similar to the experience Nisha outlined above, an existential questioning of what lies beyond this life. During this initiatory period, the shamanic practitioner can experience intense suffering and isolation. Ultimately, at its core is a severe confrontation with one's own mortality.

Although the encounter with death can happen on a psychic level as a near-death experience, often it takes place in the symbolic realms. The shamanic practitioner experiences their own death, disintegration, or dismemberment in dreams, drumming journeys, or visions. This process represents the breaking down of the old self, ego, and identity, making way for transformation and rebirth. It is a purification—a way to shed the past.

Following the symbolic death, the shaman is reborn. This rebirth signifies the creation of a new self, one that is more connected to the spiritual world and capable of accessing deeper knowledge and healing powers. Emerging with a renewed sense of purpose and spiritual insight, they have been initiated as a person who can walk between the worlds of the Dreamtime and Ordinary Reality.

Following this experience of being on the "other side" and coming back, heightened spiritual abilities may manifest in the person, including increased intuition, the ability to heal, or foreseeing future events. Traditionally, surviving and transcending the encounter with death validates the shaman's power and authenticity. It is a rite of passage that proves their worthiness and readiness to serve as a mediator between the physical and spiritual worlds.

In Siberian traditions, shamans often describe their initiation as involving a journey to the Underworld, where they are dismembered and reassembled by spirits. Many Native American shamanic traditions include vision quests or solitary retreats, during which the initiate faces death alone with the elements. In Amazonian cultures, the use of sacred plants like ayahuasca can induce visionary experiences that include encounters with death. Similarly, the peyote used by the Huichol can often bring about death-like states of consciousness.

Although plant medicines can be ingested for other purposes they can also work as a "death medicine." Used with this initiatory Intention, plant medicines take on an intense and powerful quality. Practicing death beforehand in the lucid dream realms better prepares the initiate to face the "death medicine" of psychedelics consciously and without as much fear.

The journey of death and rebirth is an archetypal experience that resonates with the human psyche. It mirrors the Hero's Journey described by mythologist Joseph Campbell, where the hero must face trials, descend into the abyss, and emerge transformed. This universal pattern underscores the shamanic path as a deeply human and transformative experience.

In this world of form and linear time it's easy to feel secure, because the laws of this world are set. We know that if we jump up, gravity will be there to pull us down. If we make money, save it up, and put it in the bank, with time we can buy stability. All this perceived stability is both our comfortable home and our prison.

That is why the Dreamtime can be simultaneously the scariest and most freeing place ever. Because it is a reality that operates with laws different from the ones in waking reality. One moment, gravity works; the next, you're flying through the atmosphere. One moment, your body is damaged and mangled; the next, you are perfectly fine. One moment, you have all the stability in the world; the next, you are swirling around in a rainbow-colored wormhole. The Dreamtime gives us a glimpse of the possibility of a reality with less solid form and non-linear time.

Some view the Dreamtime as the debris of the mind after a day in waking reality, while others see it as a cacophony of alternate dimensions. Regardless of how you see it, the Dreamtime holds a gift for you. Inside your dreams is a treasure trove of understanding about yourself and your subconscious.

Make a commitment to remember the worlds and experiences you are exploring as you sleep. As you befriend and deeply know the vast expanses of your inner world, slowly but surely, the prospect of dying and entering the ultimate unknown can become less scary. This is because you are bringing lucid awareness into the unknown of the Dreamtime, and as you do, you see that there truly is nothing to be afraid of. You become an expert in navigating the internal spaces and non-Ordinary Reality.

This is not to say that after you gain mastery in lucid dreaming you will never have moments of being afraid of death or questioning what lies beyond this life. However, as you bring conscious awareness into your dreams you will find a newfound freedom to live without a fear of death unconsciously dictating all of your decisions.

Just like the boogeyman you run from in childhood nightmares, death only grows more scary and more intense the more you fear and run from it. If you can turn and face it and earnestly ask what it wants, the answer may be that it just wants recognition. By committing to remembering and honoring the Dreamtime, you meet the presence of death in the form of the Great Unknown and can bow down before its mystery, thus befriending what once brought you great terror.

A mature practitioner of psychonavigation comes to walk in constant harmonious balance between Ordinary Reality and the Dreamtime. Aboriginal elders in Australia say that they must walk very slowly because they maintain complete awareness of both Ordinary Reality and the Dreamtime—as they walk, they must sing the song of the mountain they are passing or whisper to the bird spirits or sing to the snake on the ground. They maintain great harmony as they move through the multidimensions of time and space with this utter awareness.

You spend almost half your life dreaming, so why treat that part as if it's not of any importance? The first step to remembering your dreams is to stop saying that "It was *just* a dream" and start understanding that "It is *all* a dream."

25

Remembering Your Dreams

Fact: Everyone sleeps, everyone dreams.
Reality: Everyone sleeps, but not everyone
remembers their dreams.

Some individuals assert that they never experience dreams. However, research shows that it isn't that they aren't dreaming; rather, they aren't able to recall their dreams upon waking.

Scientists can detect when someone is dreaming based on rapid eye movements (REM) and specific brainwave patterns recorded on an electroencephalograph (EEG). When a person's eyes move rapidly during sleep, their EEG shows the corresponding brainwave pattern, and they are often able to recall a dream upon waking.

Using this method, researchers have never found anyone who doesn't dream while asleep. On average, people experience four to six dream periods each night, as established in these studies.

Now that we know that scientifically we all dream, let's explore the societal reason we may have trouble remembering our Dreamtime. From a young age, the Dreamtime is diminished and all things waking reality exalted. How many times growing up did you hear the phrase, "Oh that was *just* a dream." It could have been a parent trying to comfort you after a nightmare ("Don't worry, honey. That was just a dream. There's nothing to be afraid of") or disapproving peers putting down your ethereal encounter ("Oh, that was *just* a dream. Fairies aren't real").

Being "*just* a dream" means: It is not important and should be quickly forgotten to focus on the important things in the "reality" of waking life—the reality of paying your bills, the reality of keeping the status quo, and the reality of working all your life to achieve success and stability. One day, you can be comfortable. One day, you can be free. But that day is never quite close enough to grasp—it's always *just* around the corner.

If you hope to journey through the vast realms of your unconscious mind, you first need to establish the ability to remember what happened in your dream once you awaken. The first portal of dreaming is to remember your dreams. To bring the dreamworld into Ordinary Reality takes effort at times. This is because the membrane between waking reality and the Dreamtime can be dense, especially because the skill of remembering your dreams is not cultivated in Western-dominant culture.

Dream recollection is a constant process, rather than something you arrive at and from that point forward always remember. Even long-time lucid dreamers who have dedicated so much of their time to remembering their dreams still find that if they get lazy, they can slip right back into forgetting their dreams. The good news is that when you give the Dreamtime the focus it deserves and establish a dedicated practice of remembering, eventually your dream recall will become stronger.

Factors that May Inhibit Your Ability to Recall Your Dreams

Anxiety can be a huge inhibitor of dream recall. If something is heavy on your mind or you feel troubled about daily life concerns when you wake up, the worries may take center stage, so that you quickly forget the dream you were just having.

Ironically, your dreams hold the key to getting out from under that anxiety and solving the pressing issues in your life. Even if you wake up stressed, try to let the troubling thoughts go and return to what you were just dreaming about. Set nurturing morning routines and rituals that allow you to take the time to remember your dreams.

Some medications may also suppress your "dream sleep." Talk to your doctor to better understand what side effects your medications have and if dream suppression is one of them.

In an interesting study conducted by the *Journal of Adolescent Health*, researchers found that girls are more likely than boys to remember dreams. This fact may point to the negative cultural conditioning around connection with the emotional, non-rational world to which boys and men are subjected. Men may feel less encouraged to explore their non-rational or highly emotional worlds, thus blocking them off from the profound self-understanding those worlds hold.

Furthermore, multiple studies have found that participants who identified themselves as "creative" said that they had an easier time remembering their dreams.

If you don't think of yourself as a creative person, you may feel like you don't have access to your imagination. The dream space, much like the imagination, is a creative, non-linear world. Remember that creativity doesn't take one form or just have one meaning. We all can express our creativity in unique and compelling ways. The mere act of being alive is creative. Every day, you create new cells, new thoughts, and new projects. Creativity is not "one size fits all," so don't put yourself into a box and cut yourself off from the power of the imaginative realms. Each person must discover their particular way of accessing their powers of creativity.

It has also been found that more "psychologically minded" people, who are focused inward, remember more dreams than those who are "practical" and focused outward. This just reiterates how remembering your dreams is such a massive part of psychonavigation. When you are mindful of your inner reactions to things, rather than trying to force the external situations around you, you access a deep level of self-responsibility.

Simple Practices to Help You Remember Your Dreams

Getting enough sleep is essential for remembering your dreams

The more sleep you get, the more (and longer) REM cycles you have; the more REM cycles you have, the more likely you are to remember your dreams: You increase your chances of remembering dreams because you've had more of them.

"People tend to have most of their dream sleep in the second half of the night. If your REM sleep accounts for 20 percent of a seven-hour sleep, that's a little less than an hour and a half in total, of which you might only remember the last 10 minutes vividly," says Deborah Givan, M.D., a sleep specialist at Indiana University Health Methodist Hospital in Indianapolis.

Keeping a dream journal beside your bed is a helpful way to remember your dreams

If you want to signify to your subconscious that you are interested in hearing what it has to say, give it a physical cue, such as a dream journal, to demonstrate that you are honoring and valuing the messages it holds. Having your dream journal close by allows you to quickly capture the dream imprints before they slip away. We will discuss how to do this in the following chapter..

You may think that you'll remember a dream later in the day and put off writing it down, only to find that it is completely gone once you get around to it. If you don't have time to write down the full dream in the morning, take notes about the key moments, significant imagery, and so forth. These notes can be used to trigger your memory later on.

In *Dream on It: Unlock Your Dreams, Change Your Life*, Lauri Loewenberg writes, "The best time to try to recall your dreams is in the first 90 seconds after you wake up, before the memory goes away."[8] So, if you wake up in the middle of the night remembering a dream, it can be helpful to quickly write down or record the dream before falling back asleep.

We emphasize one final time: You are more likely to remember a dream you have freshly woken up from, so capturing the dream memory right in the moment can be extremely helpful. Now is the time to step through the first portal and remember your dreams.

26

Unlocking the Symbols and Metaphors of Your Dreams

*Since the soul's arrival in the world, it is by means
of dreams that it joyfully greets and gazes upon that
which is most beautiful and most divine.*

—PLUTARCH

Humans are not the only ones to dream. Many living organisms experience REM sleep and have dreams. It is biologically important. Dreaming provides psychic immunity to the stresses and strains of the waking state. In short, we need to dream in order to de-stress from what happened during the day.

While we sleep, our brains continue to function like computers during offline processing. They tidy up memory, merge new experiences with the old, discard outdated information, and re-label and integrate files. When we sleep, the brain switches from the verbal to the symbolic mode and continues working on issues from our waking life. That's why many times we wake up in the morning with a resolution to the problem we were stuck on the previous day.

Dreams can seem so strange from the waking point of view because a dream speaks in the language of symbols. Creating meaning in metaphors is a very economical conveyance for the brain. The function of a symbol in dreams is to communicate as clearly as possible the conception that the dreamer has in mind. In some cases, a symbol can be packed with several meanings concurrently.

The mind of the dreamer chooses certain symbols because they are identical with their notion of the referent object. There can even be multiple symbols for the same referent object. This means that the mind is capable of performing exceedingly complex operations in the Dreamtime using symbols instead of the cues the waking mind relies on. An example of how symbols can simplify processing time is the stop sign. Semiotics is a field of research into signs, symbols, and how meaning is created. The use of a red stop sign is an example of semiotics. This sign itself is a symbol that represents the concept of Stop, and is universally recognized as such. Red also signifies the concept of Danger, which adds to the overall meaning of the sign. Instead of needing a lengthy explanation or processing time to stop, we just see the stop sign and know that we must stop.

Along with symbols, dreams also have immense potential for metaphoric expression. Metaphors draw similarities between things that are different by making new and striking connections between them. That is why oftentimes our dreams may not relate directly to an issue we are facing yet hold the undercurrent of that issue within them. For example, if you are struggling with a health issue, you might dream about driving in your car and not being able to control it. Your car is a metaphor for your body, and it being out of control shows you that you feel like you don't have agency over your health.

Why do children remember dreams and integrate them daily into their creative pursuits but adults get so cut off from and distrusting of dreams? Perhaps because children live more in a world of metaphors and more in the Dreamtime, they are aware of how much they don't know and, therefore, are more able to see life by way of approximations. When we embrace approximations over definitive reality, we take on a more Taoist attitude of seeing life as an ever-unfolding mystery or the Buddhist attitude of "beginner's mind." As Spanish poet Frederic Garcia Lorca wrote, "Lord, may I be given back the child soul I once had, ripe with stories, in his feathered cap with his wooden sword."

We are so eager to define everything in a finished way, as though it's a done deal—"You are *this* to me; we are not *that*. I own *this*; *this* is mine. I am *this* and not *that*." When we live life as though everything is set in stone, it has the effect of building a wall of supposed security against the storms of change, but what would life look like if we lived it through metaphors? To answer this question, we can look to our dreams.

Metaphors in dreams usually reveal hidden aspects of our true feelings about situations in our lives. A butterfly with wings stuck together implies limited freedom; loss of a beautiful turquoise ring may represent a valued relationship slipping away—dreams tell us things we may not want to know. Therefore, a metaphoric life would be one in which we are more honest with the undercurrents of our emotions and listening to our dreams. Navigating the seas of our inner worlds as metaphoric interpreters, we can follow the admonition to "know thyself" in each moment. When we are being called upon to reinvent ourselves or escape a challenging situation, we need access to our dreams.

In 1989, dream researcher J.F. Hughes wrote in *Dreams, Myth, and Power*,[9] "Metaphors provide a bridge for the inventor between the already invented to the realm of the undiscovered." In situations where innovative viewpoints are needed, the use of metaphors and dreams are your greatest allies. Creative imagination requires us to remember that thinking in metaphors expands the mind beyond its limited habitual ways of perceiving.

Physicist Albert Einstein is often cited as having received many of his breakthroughs in dreams. Einstein had a dream in which he saw cows next to an electric fence. From his point of view, the cows all jumped up at once as they got electrocuted by the fence. However, from the perspective of the farmer standing at the other end of the fence, the cows jumped up one after another. This led him to realize that their view of the same event from different perspectives was dramatically different. It was through this dream that he formed the metaphorical connection that led him to his general theory of relativity.

English poet and literary critic Samuel Taylor Coleridge observed that for the creative imagination to work there must be a suspension of disbelief. In dreaming, we are in a state of natural suspension of belief. No matter how outlandish the situations are, we often don't question them. For example, maybe we see a pink elephant floating on a cloud and think it's the most normal thing in the world. Only when we wake up do we realize that it was, of course, a dream. When you awaken, keep the same suspension of disbelief, and approach the dream with curiosity and openness. Dreams have a way of creating unusual and impossible analogies that spur our creative imaginations into new possibilities.

With lucid dreaming, the goal is to bring a "questioning mind" into the Dreamtime. This is a mind that when viewing a pink elephant in the room asks the question "Could I be dreaming?" As we work to bridge the gap between waking reality and the Dreamtime, we hone the craft of suspending disbelief in waking reality, while also questioning the outlandish in the Dreamtime.

It's both exciting and humbling to pay attention to our dreams. The language of dreams can seem confusing or even scary or ridiculous sometimes, and we often even need help in understanding our own dream metaphors. Dream interpretation can be a profound tool for self-exploration and personal growth, allowing you to delve into the subconscious mind to uncover hidden truths, unresolved issues, and creative insights.

Dreams are unique to each person; therefore, interpreting your own dreams is crucial for maintaining personal empowerment and authenticity. Too often people become overly dependent on the interpretations of others for their dreams. They will run to dream dictionaries before spending enough time listening to the dream messages for themselves.

Relying on others or generic online dream dictionaries can dilute the personal significance of your dreams and lead to misinterpretation. While these sources can offer general insights, they often lack the nuance necessary to fully grasp the unique messages your subconscious is conveying.

Handing over the responsibility of interpreting your dreams to others can lead to a loss of personal power and agency. Dreams are intimate communications from your inner self, and only you possess the full context and emotional resonance to decode their meanings accurately. External interpretations can impose meanings that do not resonate with your personal experiences, potentially leading to confusion or misguided decisions.

When You Interpret Your Dreams, You Engage in an Element of Psychonavigation

The act of writing down and dissecting the messages of your dream life is a charting of your inner worlds. By tracking your dreams in this way, you can create your own "dream dictionary," personalized to your dream symbols. Doing this is a crucial element of developing your lucid dreaming practice. If you diligently write down your dreams you will begin to see patterns and be able to decode your dream symbols for yourself.

For example, you might dream about spiders over and over again. Seeing what emotional experience the spider evokes, what other situations surround the spider in your dream, and what is going on in your waking life, you may come to realize that for *you* the spider is an indicator of a big transformation that is about to come. This might not be the case for someone else who sees a spider in their dreams; it is your personal metaphor.

While it is essential to do the work of interpreting your dreams yourself, discussing them with trusted friends, family, or therapists can be beneficial. Speaking your dreams aloud can help clarify your thoughts and reveal insights you might not have noticed on your own. It allows you to explore different perspectives and deepen your understanding. However, remember that the final interpretation should come from you, as you are the ultimate authority on your inner world.

Steps for Personal Dream Interpretation

- **Record Your Dreams** – Keep a dream journal by your bedside, and write down your dreams as soon as you wake up. Include as many details as possible, focusing on emotions, symbols, and recurring themes.
- **Reflect on Your Life Context** – What is happening in your waking life that might influence your dreams? Look for connections between your dream content and your current thoughts, feelings, and experiences.

- **Identify Key Symbols** – Highlight and track significant symbols in your dreams. Reflect on what they mean to you personally. Avoid relying on generic definitions; instead, think about what these symbols represent in your life.
- **Explore Emotions** – Pay attention to the emotions you experienced in your dream. Strong emotions with particular symbols within the dream can point to unresolved issues you are currently facing.
- **Deepen your study of dream symbols through drumming journeys** – When you go on a drumming journey ask your power animal to guide you to the deeper meaning of a particular dream. Let the power of the trance state that drumming induces lead you back into the dream material to better understand it.

Embrace the journey of psychonavigation by taking time to interpret your dreams. You must use your dreams as a guide to navigate the depths of your psyche and uncover the wisdom within.

27

Tracking Training for Lucid Dreaming

As discussed in the previous chapter, remembering your dreams is a practice. It takes a willingness to dedicate some of your time and mental energy to prioritizing your dreamworld. As noted, one key way to signal to your subconscious that you care about the Dreamtime is by keeping a dream journal. Allow writing in your dream journal to be a special gift you give yourself each morning.

Even if you cannot dedicate every morning to writing down your dreams, at least make time to write down your dreams several times a week. On mornings when you don't have time to write down your dream, as suggested, jot down a few notes about the dream then when you have more time go back and write out the rest of it.

You might not understand the significance of a dream until much later but valuing each dream that you have will train your memory to hold onto them once the morning comes. Keeping a dream journal doesn't need to be a huge production.

An Easy Way to Structure Your Dream Journal

- **Write down the date** – Dating your dream will help you look back at your dreams and see what they foreshadowed in your life. You gain a deeper understanding of the dreams retroactively.
- **Write down your dream** – Write down as much of your dream as you can remember, even if it's a description of just a few sentences. By continually making a practice of writing down your dreams, you will find that you remember more and more of your dreams. Sometimes, as you are writing, you may even find

that you recall more in the moment. One word can trigger a flood of dream images and elements.

- **Give your dream a title** – After you've written down as much as you can remember, name your dream. Naming your dream is a great way to both summarize your overall experience of the dream as well as provide a system to easily go back and find dreams to revisit.
- **Write down any emotions** – Write down the emotions you had during the dream or ones you experienced after waking up from the dream. What is the overall tone of the dream you just woke up from? Sometimes the dream itself may seem insignificant, but you wake up feeling a strong emotion. The emotional tone may make more sense as time progresses and you look back on a particular dream and the message it was revealing to you.
- **Underline parts that stand out to you** – Go through your dream and see if there are any moments or elements that feel especially potent. Even if you don't logically understand why they are important, trust your intuition, and underline them for later assessment. For example, you may have a dream in which you are bitten by a snake. Even if you don't know why it's important that a snake bit you, underline that moment. You can take it a step further by researching the meaning of snake bites in different traditions and see if that adds to the significance of your dream. Make notes in the margins or on the next page about what is revealed to you from the underlined parts. Days or months later, when you revisit a dream, add any other notes about the significance that has been revealed.
- **Note what kind of dream it was** – There are indeed different types of dreams and different levels of lucidity within them. According to the Tibetan Buddhist framework, there are everyday *samsaric dreams*, *dreams of clarity*, and *clear light dreams*:

- Samsaric dreams are the ones most regularly experienced. These result from "karmic traces," or the sorting out and reactions to the material of the day and can also be viewed as ordinary dreams—the mind is swept here and there without much agency or order.
- Dreams of clarity are much more transformational. These dreams have a more vivid and impactful quality to them.
- Clear light dreams are ones in which the dreamer is the clear light of the mind and free from dreams, thoughts, and images.
- Another way of categorizing the different levels of dreams is *non-lucid, semi-lucid,* and *fully lucid*:
  - Non-lucid dreams are ones in which the dreamer has no sense that they are dreaming and interacts with the dream as if it were not a dream.
  - Semi-lucid dreams are ones in which the dreamer has a sense that they *might* be dreaming but does not become fully lucid. They are also dreams where the dreamer wakes up after the dream and thinks they may have known they were dreaming at some point in the dream.
  - Fully lucid dreams are ones in which the dreamer knows beyond a doubt that they are dreaming and, as such, can interact with the dream material with more agency.
  Noting the kind of dream can help you notice patterns in your lucid dreaming practice and the frequency of the various types of dreams.

Bonus — Use Another Divination Tool, such as the Tarot

One other thing you can do after writing down your dream is to pull tarot cards for the dream to elaborate or expand on its meaning. Pull one card for the overall meaning of the dream, or several cards related to certain elements of the dream. Divination of this sort can provide an extra element of insight and deeper meaning. Record the cards you pulled and a brief summary of their meaning under your dream entry. We have created *Lucid Dreaming, Lucid Living: Your Oracle and Guide to Mastering the Dreamscape* specifically to work with lucid dreaming. You can use this oracle deck to help unlock the messages of your dreams.

Dream Signs

Another thing you will want to begin tracking is your personal "dream signs." A dream sign is a recurring event, situation, space, or object that appears in your dreams repetitively. When you write down your dreams, like a skilled hunter, you can track what recurrent elements they present and uncover the dream signs that often appear in your dreams.

These themes or elements in your dreams are often related to waking-reality situations, spaces, or events you interact with. Identifying these signs is a crucial step toward recognizing when you are in a dream state. When you discover your dream signs you can use them to gain lucidity.

By analyzing your dream journal, you can note recurring symbols or scenarios and become aware of your unique dream signs. After a few weeks of journaling, review your entries for common patterns, highlighting or listing recurring people, places, or events.

Creating a dream sign catalog can serve as a quick reference, allowing you to recognize these signs more easily while you are actually dreaming. Organize your dream signs into categories such as Places, People, Actions, and Objects. This methodical approach will help you spot dream signs more readily and serve as prompts that you are dreaming.

Examples of recurring dream signs include: being in an elevator, standing near the ocean, seeing a deceased loved one or pet, being back in high school, performing on stage but not knowing any of your lines, traveling on a plane or bus, and many more.

One of NISHA'S Dream Signs

I have a particularly funny dream sign: being in the bathroom. For whatever reason, countless times in my dreams, I find myself in the bathroom. It's usually not a very clean or enjoyable bathroom, either. Although this might seem like a strange dream anomaly, to just "write off," recognizing this as a dream sign for myself has led to more lucid dream experiences than I can count. Making use of this dream sign, whenever I am in a bathroom in waking reality I stop to ask myself: "Am I dreaming?" By performing this regular action of questioning whether or not I am dreaming in my daily life, this leads to lucidity in my dream life. Thus, dirty bathrooms, ironically, can make me lucid.

Dream signs are unique to each person, so each person has to find their distinct dream signs. How you do this is by going back through your dreams and highlighting recurring elements that appear. You will start to see a pattern emerging of elements that show up in your dreams.

Don't write off your dream signs. There aren't any "bad" or "stupid" dream signs. They are all tools to trigger lucidity and help you realize that you are dreaming!

Assignment: Collect Your Dream Signs

After dream journaling for a couple of weeks to a month, go back and highlight each dream sign you can find. On a separate page (perhaps in the back of your dream journal), write down all of the dream signs you find. You can continue to add to this list as you amass more dream signs.

Performing State Checks

When you encounter a dream sign, perform what is called a "state check," or "reality check." This is a test you perform during the day to determine whether you are awake or dreaming. Making state checks a habit increases the likelihood of performing them in a dream and thus attaining lucidity.

Common state checks include looking at your hands (as hands often appear distorted in dreams), pinching your nose and trying to breathe through it (if you can breathe, you're likely dreaming); reading a piece of text, looking away, and reading it again (text often changes upon a second glance in dreams); or jumping up and seeing if you can fly (if you are dreaming you normally can fly).

The most well-known state check is looking at your hands. This can partially be credited to Castaneda's writings, because that was a task given to him by his teacher Don Juan—to find his hands within the dream. The action of finding one's hands in the dream was considered the First Gate of Dreaming.

It did not come easily to Castaneda to find his hands. When he eventually did see his hands in the dream state, he asked Don Juan why he gave him that particular task. Interestingly, Don Juan told him that the action of finding his hands was rather arbitrary, and it could have been anything else. More than the action, it was about getting Castaneda to find his dreaming attention. This dreaming attention can be viewed as the focus that it takes to become lucid. One must be present enough within the dream to remember the Intent or task they are carrying over from waking reality.

One way to strengthen that Intent and dreaming attention is to pay the same amount of present attention in waking life. Every time you notice a dream sign in waking reality you ask yourself "Could I be dreaming?" and perform a state check to see if you are dreaming. By making this a regular habit, you train your mind to always question if you could be dreaming when you encounter one of your dream signs.

Recognizing a dream sign often triggers the realization that one is in a dream. Since these are things that regularly appear in your dreams, eventually you ask the question "Could I be dreaming?" while in a dream. Once you do that, perform a state check to see if you're dreaming. If you are indeed dreaming, you will become lucid!

Frequently practicing the performance of state checks is essential to lucid dreaming. Engaging in one each time you see a dream sign is a great way to reinforce the habit. This all culminates in a more accurate knowledge of your personal dream symbology and signs.

Through familiarizing yourself with what appears in your dreams, you begin to understand your own unique dream symbol system. Understanding the qualities of the various realities you venture into (waking or asleep) helps you to become lucid when in the dream state.

You can also set reminders on your phone to encourage you to perform state checks. Furthermore, you can associate state checks with routine activities, such as every time you check the time or walk through a door. All of these regular reminders can help integrate this practice into your daily life.

> NISHA'S **Example of Using a Dream Sign and State Check to Become Lucid**
>
> I was hanging out with a friend and had to go to the bathroom. When I got there, the light switch wouldn't work. I looked in the mirror and could barely see myself. It was strange that the light wouldn't switch on—I had the thought that maybe I was dreaming. But no, I thought, this is so real, I can't be dreaming. And yet, since bathrooms were one of my dreams signs, I thought I might as well try jumping up, so I did. Sure enough, I stayed in the air for an extended amount of time! I laughed to myself because it felt so real, so much like I was awake, but I was in fact dreaming. I became fully lucid and flew out of the bathroom.

Writing in a Waking Journal

Just as it is important to remember what happens in your dreamworld, it is also valuable to remember what happens in waking life by writing it down in a waking journal at the end of the day. To become a fully whole person, we must collect our personal power through strengthening the memory of our life, rather than let it pass us by unconsciously.

Did you ever lie down in bed and before falling asleep try to remember everything that happened during the day? Maybe you realized with shock and horror that you couldn't even remember everything that happened just a few hours ago.

It's amazing how fickle memory can be. Even recent memories can get thrown out by the mind if deemed not important enough. Perhaps our memory is fickle because modern humans do not value memory, do not practice memory, and do not cultivate the ability to remember.

Working with lucid dreaming requires a great deal of memory. You must remember to check if you are dreaming, remember the particular goals you have for your lucid dreaming practice, and remember your dream once you wake up. Crossing between waking and dreaming states, one seems to go through a veil of forgetting. Even for practiced lucid dreamers, once in a lucid dream it can be easy to forget what you wanted to do once lucid.

Navigating your psyche requires that you remember what you encounter in each phase of consciousness. Strengthening your memory requires strengthening your presence in each moment. By taking the time to recall your life each day, you strengthen:

- Your memory, which will help you remember your days as well as your dreams at night.
- Your ability to analyze the events of the day and look for "dream signs" in your waking life.
- Your insight into how the events of the day are impacting your subconscious and psyche at night.
- Your knowledge of self. When you write in a waking journal what occurred during the day as well as your internal process surrounding the events, you can study what progress you've made in habitual ways of acting and where you remain stuck.

In a sense, by writing about your day in a waking journal before bed, you are clearing your mind of the debris of the day. It is an especially helpful practice if you notice that many of your dreams feel like clutter and worries from the day before. Clearing out your mind, you make space for more transformational rather than "karmic" everyday dreams.

When formatting your waking journal you can take a similar approach to your dream journal. By aligning the recollection of the two worlds you are entraining your mind to constantly be observant and present.

By studying your waking reality for strange occurrences, dream signs, and synchronicities, you are training your mind to constantly check in with what phase of consciousness you are in: waking or dreaming. Thus, your mind is entrained to be lucid.

An Easy Way to Structure Your Waking Journal

- **Write down the date** – By tracking each day, you can go back and review the days from a higher perspective, seeing not just what was going on in one moment or one day but the patterns that appear over weeks and months.
- **Write down your day** – Similar to writing down your dream, try to write as much of your day as you can remember. When you start each day knowing that you will try to recall it in the evening, you train your mind to be present and store information rather than forget events almost immediately after they happen.
- **Give your day a title** – After you've written down as much of your day as you can remember, name your day. Similar to naming your dream, naming your day is a great way to both summarize the overall experience of the day as well as provide a system to easily go back and find days to revisit.
- **Write down any emotions** – Within each day, you may experience a plethora of emotions. Write down all you experienced. You can write them under specific chunks of the day where they appeared or all at the end of your day summary. Doing this, you can also see if there are emotions that carry through from the day into the Dreamtime and if some emotions

from the Dreamtime stick with you throughout the day. You can even chart your emotions from one day to the next, as you amass more and more waking journal entries.

- **Underline parts that stand out to you** – Oftentimes, the parts of the day we remember are the moments that are particularly shocking or evoke strong emotions. By collecting your full day as much as possible, you can review and underline both the obviously "charged" moments as well as more subtle ones that seem significant upon review. Another great thing to do is revisit entries and underline parts that, in the moment didn't seem important, but with time are revealed to be deeply "telling."
- **Studying the Shadow** – Using the Outer/Inner Chart format can be very helpful for tracking how the Shadow pattern is showing up in your daily life. When someone irritates or triggers you in some way, make sure to note your reactions, then later sit down to write the Outer/Inner chart of this incident in your journal.

Bonus

Just as you can pull tarot cards in the morning to give insight into your dreams, it is also helpful to pull a card in the evening after you write down your day. This card can be used as a summary of the energetic tone of the day or insight into an element of the day that you may have missed.

28

Attaining and Maintaining Lucidity

Now that you have a solid foundation of dream recall, dream-sign tracking, and state checks, you are ready to work on attaining lucidity. Within the realms of working with your psyche, setting a clear Intent is the way to focus your willpower on the desired outcome. Think of your Intent as an arrow launched at the target of lucidity. The more focused you are when drawing your bow to shoot your arrow, the better your chances of hitting your target.

However, as with shooting an arrow, it takes practice to become a master archer. Don't shoot it once, miss, and get discouraged. By letting loose the arrow of your Intent repeatedly, and with diligence, soon you will hit the mark of lucidity.

Before you go to bed set the clear Intent that you will become lucid. One name for this technique is Mnemonically Induced Lucid Dreaming (MILD). Before falling asleep, you repeat a phrase like "I will realize that I'm dreaming" while visualizing yourself becoming lucid in a dream. This technique leverages the power of suggestion and visualization. Take yourself on a guided journey much like you do in drumming journeys. You can even implement a similar pattern that you take in drumming journeys to "walk down" into the lucid dream state.

Set your mind to a task like digging a tunnel while holding the focus on retaining lucidity when you fall asleep. Imagine that the dream material is on the other side of the tunnel that you are digging. Imagine yourself reaching a door. This is the portal into the dream. Open the door, and on the other side is the dream. Examine and explore it and then ask yourself, "Could I be dreaming?" Imagine yourself performing a state check, such as jumping in the air. You are in a dream, so you float up into the sky. Now imagine what you'd like to do once you become lucid, and do it! Through this technique, you are creating patterned pathways in your mind toward lucidity.

Navigating in the lucid realms is incredibly freeing and euphoric. The first portal of dreamwork is remembering your dreams. The second portal is remembering to check if you are dreaming and thus become lucid.

Another method to become lucid within a dream is the Wake Back to Bed (WBTB) technique. This involves waking up after 4–6 hours of sleep, staying awake for 15–30 minutes while engaging in a quiet activity like reading about lucid dreaming, then returning to sleep with the Intention to become lucid. This method increases the likelihood of entering REM sleep, where lucid dreams are most common.

Through this technique, you are jumping back into the dream space. This technique aligns with a polyphasic sleep schedule. Rather than staying in the Dreamtime throughout the whole night, you are dipping into the dream state, then back out, then back in again. Moving between the Dreamtime and Ordinary Reality, you create a crossover of the two and thus enhance your chances of becoming lucid.

If you struggle with insomnia or falling back asleep once you've woken up, this might not be the best technique for you. Setting aside a period of time, perhaps a lucid dreaming vacation or retreat, where you are also able to nap throughout the day, can be another great way to engage with this technique.

Beyond these techniques, the most important thing you can do for lucid dreaming is the practice of questioning what reality or phase of consciousness you are in during the day. You are developing a "questioning mind" that is constantly asking if you could be asleep or awake. Within the discipline of learning psychonavigation, you are training your psyche to remain astute and aware in each moment as to where it is in relation to the map of Ordinary Reality and the Dreamtime.

The questioning mind is naturally offline when you are in the dreamworld. Strengthening the muscle of keenly observing your reality to see what state of consciousness you are in, increases the chance of asking the question at the right time—when you are dreaming. When you ask that question in a dream, you are bringing the questioning mind back online. Once that part of your awareness is reactivated, you must remember to perform a state check. State checks are what help you to know beyond a doubt whether or not you are dreaming. A road block for some people is that they get to the stage of questioning, but then the dream material is so convincing that they fool themselves into thinking it's not a dream. That is why state checks are your main ally in becoming lucid.

Some people fear that they will become confused about Ordinary Reality and the Dreamtime as they engage in these practices—that the lines will blur. However, by performing state checks and studying the various states (Ordinary Reality and the Dreamtime), you become *more* aware of the distinctions between the various states. Lucid dreaming indeed feels very real, as real as waking reality, but it has a different quality than waking reality. Of course, if you have mental health issues that could lead to confusion in distinguishing between Ordinary Reality and the Dreamtime, you should work closely with your therapist when engaging in lucid dreaming work. Together, assess if it is the right path for you.

Take on the task of checking your reality regularly. Watch for signs of what state of consciousness you are in. Is there something strange happening in your immediate environment? Perform a state check. Are you experiencing an event that normally occurs in your Dreamtime? Perform a state check. Each time you question if you could be dreaming, do it earnestly. Chances are that you will be pleasantly surprised when you ask the question (even though you suspect you are not dreaming) only to perform a state check and find that you actually are!

Maintaining Lucidity

Once you realize with elation that you are dreaming, it can be easy to become so surprised or excited you wake yourself up. For many beginning lucid dreamers, this can be a frustrating next challenge of lucid dreaming—remaining lucid and staying in the lucid dream.

Being able to maintain lucidity is a core skill for navigating your psyche. It's all about keeping your focused attention on the present moment. Much like in a meditation practice, the mind likes to wander and easily becomes distracted.

Drumming journeys help you practice maintaining lucidity because they enforce your ability to focus the mind. Trance states put you in a place between the worlds, where you are still aware of your physical body in waking reality and can move it around at any moment. Much like having a foot in both Ordinary Reality and the Dreamtime you have some awareness of each world and are dipping your consciousness into the Dreamtime while still anchored in waking reality.

When you fully enter the Dreamtime through sleep, this is less true as you are more cut off from your physical body and the Ordinary Reality where your body is resting. For this reason, practicing retaining lucidity through drumming journeys is an excellent introduction to dreaming lucidly in the Dreamtime.

Remember that setting your mind a task, such as digging within a drumming journey, helps bring it back on track when it gets distracted. When you are on the drumming journey, you find and follow your power animal. This builds the skill of aligning with your inner guidance system. Having developed the ability to follow your inner guidance system also comes in handy when lucid dreaming, because you are building trust with yourself that you will only venture to places within your psyche where you are ready to go. Sometimes, lucid dreaming can become scary or overwhelming because of how real it feels. Dealing with your past wounds through drumming journeys can better prepare you to face them in lucid dreams. They also foretell what challenging shadows you may encounter in your dream realms.

As stated, sometimes lucid dreams take on the quality of Upper World journeys more than Underworld ones. In this space you can accomplish extraordinary feats impossible in waking reality, such as walking through walls, breathing underwater, flying, and shape-shifting. You may also encounter beings of great power, such as deities, your higher self, and unitive consciousness. By doing the shadow excavation work in the Underworld through drumming journeys, you are building the impeccability to be able to handle these Upper World experiences without becoming too egotistical.

When you draw from the lessons gained through drumming journeys, it becomes less challenging to maintain lucidity in dreams. If you feel your lucidity beginning to slip away, focus on an object in the dream. It could be anything, but the floor is often a good area of focus because it grounds you in the dream. Keeping a single-pointed focus on the ground will help you stay lucid in your dream. When you focus on an object, you are engaging with the dream material deeply. Keeping any item in sight in the dream brings the wandering mind back into focused lucidity. Much like refocusing on the task of digging, you are giving the mind something to do in the present moment.

Another way to regain lucidity is to spin around within the dream. When a dream begins to fade, some senses remain longer than others. Often, physical sensations are the last to go, whereas one of the first to go is visual perception—the dream might lose color and begin to fade into darkness.

As soon as the dream begins to fade, start spinning using your dream body. It can be a little tricky to get the hang of spinning in a dream; however, it is a very helpful technique to bring back lucidity. When you spin, the dream reforms itself around you; you can even use it to transport yourself into another dreamscape. You do this by starting to spin and imagining where you would like to be once you stop spinning. Remind yourself that you are dreaming while you spin to retain lucidity.

NISHA'S Example of Spinning to Maintain Lucidity

I was traveling in a city with my friend, and as we were walking in one of the tall, old buildings, I had a feeling that I might be dreaming. I looked at some of the people in the city, and they seemed strange. I was sure that I was dreaming and became lucid.

I busted out one of the large screen windows in the building and told my friend that we were dreaming and she needed to believe me. I beckoned her to come with me and then took the leap. Sure enough I could fly, although not very high—more like large leaps. She laughed and followed me.

The dream began to fade as I felt my body move in my bed. No, I thought, I want to keep dreaming.

I began to spin in the dream. At first, it was hard, but I kept doing it more and more. The dream re-formed around me. I was in a new location in a boat house. I laughed, happy that spinning had worked to keep me in the lucid dream. I spun around again to transport myself to another dream scene. It was a desert. I kept spinning and taking myself to different dream locations while maintaining lucidity.

According to Stephen LaBerge, who has conducted many scientific studies on lucid dreaming, spinning may work on a neurophysiological level. Head and body movement are monitored by the vestibular system of the inner ear (which is what helps you keep balance). This system is closely integrated with visual information so that the brain can produce a stable picture of reality as you move, rather than the world shaking every time you walk.

There is a high likelihood that the same brain systems are activated when you are spinning in a dream because of how real the visual stimuli of the dream are. Neuroscientists have obtained indirect evidence that the vestibular system is involved in the production of REM bursts in sleep. Therefore, it could be hypothesized that the spinning technique works with the ear balance mechanisms to push you back into REM sleep.

LaBerge goes on to explain another reason spinning might work is that when you engage with one sense within the dream, your sensitivity to external stimuli of your sleeping body decreases. This is similar to the technique of focusing on an object in the dream. You are engaging your senses deeply in the dream and thus withdrawing them from your physical body. Oftentimes, your physical body will be what pulls you out of a lucid dream. You feel yourself moving and wake up, so pulling your attention away from your physical body helps you stay in the dream.

Along with a physical body, you have a dream body. The concept of a dream body (or astral body) is present in multiple lineages such as those of Buddhists, Naguals, and Theosophists. Lucid dreaming and astral projection are ways to build up the energy within your dream body.

The dream body could also be viewed as a vehicle for psychonavigation, because it is the body that can travel out of Ordinary Reality into the liminal dream realms. As the dream body amasses more energy by you bringing your lucid awareness to it, it can become more solid and formed. Think of it as recharging your dream body. By engaging with your senses in a lucid dream, you are perceiving them through your dream body and thus, keeping yourself in that body rather than returning to your waking body.

Now that you've learned how to achieve and sustain lucidity, you're ready to explore the transformative potential of lucid dreaming to engage with your psyche.

29

Dealing with the Shadow in the Dream Realms

When you wake up from a horrible nightmare and realize that it was "only a dream," a wave of relief washes over you. That is because you can recognize that whatever was happening, no matter how intense, does not have waking-life consequences. In a sense, you have escaped from the trappings of your mind and awoken into a new, better reality.

The act of becoming lucid within a nightmarish dream can have the same effect of bringing great relief. You switch from being involved and tormented by the dream material to "waking up" within the dream and seeing that whatever is happening isn't "real" and cannot hurt you.

Unlike when you just wake yourself up from a nightmare, when you become lucid within the nightmare and stay in it, you have a profound opportunity. You can deal directly with the nightmarish situation that your psyche presented you in a whole new way. Knowing that you cannot be physically hurt or killed within the dream, you can step into a new level of empowerment and face the frightening situations head on. Through studying the fears that are arising directly you are in a sense studying the Shadow material arising within you.

Astutely tracking and studying your nightmares can happen regardless of whether or not you are lucid in the dream state. Rather than looking at nightmares as random or just there to disturb you, as a psychonavigator you can leverage them as an excellent way to study the Shadow.

When nightmares are occurring in your life, take time to write them down. Collect your nightmare material, and look for recurring themes, emotions, and characters that regularly appear. The Dreamtime is symbolic, so the material of the nightmares may not clearly be linked to the Shadow elements that are present in your waking reality. However, when you amass a collection of nightmares to study, you will most likely see a pattern emerge that points to deeper wounds in your psyche calling out for healing.

Similar to nightmares, recurring dreams can also present a prime opportunity to study the Shadow. You can think of a recurring dream as a loop within your mind that your consciousness is stuck replaying over and over again. Often, the reason why this looping recurrent theme is happening is that your psyche is seeking resolution.

As long as you remain in a non-lucid state, it will be difficult to come all the way through to resolution. In this case, a non-lucid state can either mean the inability to become lucid within your dream or the inability to seek a lucid resolution while awake.

This is to say, that even if you cannot become lucid within the dream and work through the recurring situation, you can still work with it in a lucid way once you wake up. By taking on dreamwork as an opportunity to deal with the Shadow and study it, you are bringing the healing power of lucidity into your Dreamtime.

How to Remain Lucid Within a Nightmare or Recurring Dream

Remaining lucid within a nightmare can be a daunting task. When you are in a heightened, fearful state within a dream, the realization that you are dreaming can often lead to the immediate desire to wake up. In fact, many people realize that they are dreaming through scary encounters in the Dreamtime, and it is a natural reaction to "flee" from that fearful encounter and wake oneself up.

As you strengthen your ability to lucid-dream with regularity, you will better prepare yourself to stay lucid in nightmares. When you know how to extend lucidity, you can resist the urge to jump back into waking reality. When you encounter a frightful situation in your dream and have the thought *Could I be dreaming?* immediately perform a "state check" to confirm that you are dreaming. Once you confirm that it's a dream, let yourself feel the relief of knowing that nothing can hurt your physical body, no matter how scary the scene is. There is no death in the

Dreamtime, so you can know that ultimately you are safe and have the power to face what is being presented.

From the Dream Yoga worldview, after you die, the mind creates various visions, both beautiful and frightening, for you to face. If you can realize that they are nothing more than the material of a dream (illusions) you can dissolve the illusions of the mind and come into clear awareness. However, if you get sucked into the illusions and delusions, you suffer needlessly at the hands of your own mind. Thus, working with nightmares in a lucid state is the perfect practice to prepare the mind not to get stuck after death.

Realizing that the material of the nightmare is a creation of your psyche being presented for you to heal, you can liberate yourself from its clutches rather than suffering needlessly in its grasp. The nightmare loses power over you, because the only real power it had was the power you gave to it in the first place.

Recurring dreams can also be used as fodder for your lucid dreaming practice. Oftentimes, they are a perfect "dream sign" because they are a situation that regularly happens in your dream. Recurring dreams can be similar to nightmares in that they contain uncomfortable or troubling situations. They may not be as extreme as nightmares but can still be disturbing or challenging.

Many people have the recurring dream of being back in school and having to give a presentation. In a non-lucid state, this could continue to be an uncomfortable dream pattern. However, when a lucid dreamer encounters this situation, they will recognize that this is something they often dream about. They will take a moment to pause and do a state check, and when they do, lucidity will be theirs. Lucid dreamers are like skilled hunters of the Dreamtime—always looking for tracks and signs that they could be dreaming.

Studying the Shadow as It Appears in Your Life

When you have a nightmare, it is often pointing to a Shadow in your waking reality. The first thing to do is to study what is currently irritating or troubling you in your life. After that you will be able to see the crossover of how this Shadow pattern is entering your dreams in a symbolic way.

As you've learned, within the Journey to Completion methodology, Shadow study takes place by examining Shadow material in a particular way. You look at both the Outer Shadow and Inner Shadow. Together, they create the whole Shadow pattern. One could not exist without the other—like two pieces of a puzzle, they fit together.

Studying the Shadow in Nightmares and Recurring Dreams

Study the Outer Shadows in your waking life, you can gather a handful of nightmares and begin your Shadow study of them. Look at the nightmare material and what is happening and write down the Outer Shadow qualities. If it is a person who is acting in horrible ways, write down their qualities. For example, if in your nightmare you are being chased by a murderer, how are they acting? Are they cold, heartless, relentless? Write down all of those qualities. Now, look at how you react to them. Are you helpless, exhausted, hopeless? Write down those qualities, as they are your Inner Shadow.

As you study multiple nightmares, chances are that you will see a pattern emerge between the qualities of the Outer Shadow people or situations and your Inner Shadow reactions. Even if the nightmares are vastly different, the symbolic qualities they embody and your reaction to them will probably be similar. By conducting a Shadow study of your nightmares, you are gathering the insights into your psyche that they are presenting.

Along with nightmares, recurring dreams can be studied in the same way. Look at what the outer situations and people are doing in your recurring dreams, and see how you react to them. Write down what you find, and collect the challenging material your mind is unearthing for you to be healed and transmuted.

You don't have to be able to lucid-dream in order to study the Shadow material within your nightmares. Once you do become lucid, however, there are wonderful healing things you can do within the dream itself. These include the following measures:

Turn and Face What You Are Running From

In a nightmare, once you become lucid, you can stop running from the monster or troubling situation that is tormenting you. In a lucid state, knowing that nothing can hurt you, take a non-dualist view of the dream material. Once you exit the paradigm that whatever is causing fear in your dream is evil, you can face it squarely. For example, if you are running from a monster, stop running and instead, ask what it wants. The insights from this conversation can be deeply healing and profound.

Set Strong Boundaries

Sometimes a conversation with what or who is scaring you is not possible, even when you are lucid-dreaming. In this case, what your psyche is calling you to do is set stronger boundaries. This can be especially true in sleep paralysis states. It is a common experience to half wake up and yet not be able to move your body, often accompanied by seeing a frightening figure standing over you or holding you down.

When you become lucid in this state, you can set strong boundaries with these figures. Knowing that ultimately you have a great deal of power and control within the lucid dream realms, you can put up a strong boundary. Tell the energies that you do not wish to deal with them. You can even shoot out a blazing golden light from the palms of your hands or envision a golden circle around you that they cannot pass through. Using your dream voice is also a profound way to set boundaries, letting out a lion's roar of "No!" or "Leave!" in order to push the visions away. Setting boundaries like this in your dream space has the powerful effect of enabling you to set strong boundaries in your waking life, too.

Call on Your Allies

Now that you have experience calling on your power animal allies in drumming journeys, you understand how important it is to have allies in the Dreamtime. If you are facing intense fears in the Dreamtime, call on allies to help you. Summoning allies once you become lucid is a great way to gather your power.

Envision who or what you would like to come join you. You could call out to your higher self, your power animal, and deities you have a connection with, such as Jesus, Buddha, or any other powerful energies that hold personal significance for you.

Once you have the energy of your ally with you in your dream, you will find that the nightmare energy is no longer able to overcome you in the same way. Just as you need allies in the Dreamtime to deal with nightmares, it is also wise to have allies in waking reality, such as a therapist, close friend, or family member, who can help you process the work you are doing with your nightmares and past traumas.

Nightmare Rewrite Technique

Even if you are not able to become lucid within the nightmare, we have developed a technique to help you use the energy of the nightmare to reenter the dream in a lucid way. Just like descending into the Underworld during a drumming journey, you can revisit the nightmare in your imagination after waking to heal what it revealed.

When you wake up from a nightmare, often your mind will continue to replay the material from it over and over again. This unpleasant process is the mind trying to deal with what you just experienced but instead, getting stuck in a fearful loop. Rather than just sleeplessly lying in bed troubled by your dream, use this natural spinning of the mind to your advantage.

When you "reimagine" the dream, you are moving into that state of consciousness between Ordinary Reality and the Dreamtime wherein your brain wave patterns shift and you are experiencing the dream quality of consciousness yet lucid within it.

After years of working with nightmares lucidly, we created the following technique to work with them:

- When you wake up from a nightmare, think back to the most troubling part.
- Repeat to yourself that it was a dream, and therefore, you can become lucid within it and deal with the material in a lucid way.
- Close your eyes and imagine yourself back in the nightmare at the most troubling or challenging part, but this time you have lucidity. You know that nothing can hurt you, and you are here to heal what is being presented.
- Call on your ally to assist you. Again, this can be your higher self, power animal, and so on. Picture them standing next to you.
- Next, imagine yourself imbued with the powerful energy of lucidity. You can even picture white or golden light surrounding you.
- If there were people being harmed by the Outer Shadow of the nightmare go and heal them. For example, if someone was stabbed by a killer in your dream, go over to them, and imagine a blue light healing their wounds. Rather than seeing them as victimized by the Outer Shadow, you see them in a space beyond human mortality. Let them take on a form beyond death where they are in their light bodies.
- Look at whatever is harming you or causing fear within the dream, and strip away its outer form. In this step, you are calling in "non-dualistic consciousness." Rather than seeing them as evil or bad, you are peeling back the layers of projection to see a core vision of the energy behind them. For example, if it was an evil person, you can imagine peeling away their form to reveal what is beneath.
- At this point, you will often find that you are back in the dream, rather than "just imagining" what is happening. You have rendered the dream with full lucid awareness.

- Having resolved the dualities being presented by your psyche, talk to the shadowy character in your dream and help them move beyond their troubling behavior.
- What happens next is oftentimes unexpected and unique to the dream. However, you have recovered your power and lucidly dealt with what was transpiring in the dream.

Example of a Nightmare Rewrite from NISHA'S Dream

In my dream, I was watching a TV show about a stepfather who was really mean to his son and punished him in harsh ways. I changed the channel, then later, I came back to the show to check on how the boy was doing.

He was sitting in the circle, and he didn't look that hurt from the outside, but I could tell he was damaged. I changed the channel once again, then came back to the show, and he was even more beaten down.

I started to wake up when the mean stepfather was coming back for him. No, I thought. I will rewrite this.

This time I went back into the show in the dream fully lucid. The son was too beaten down to fight back. As the abusive man approached, I stood my ground in front of him. I floated up into the air to prove that I was lucid. I did a state check with my hands as well.

The man threatened me and told me to get out of the way. I stood still, protecting the son. When the cruel man came close to me I sent out an electrifying touch, and the human form of his arm fell away to reveal a glowing blue light body. He kept coming at me, and I kept touching his different limbs to reveal the blue light until he only had one leg.

He was angry and cursing me, and I told him to remember who he was. I was still floating up in the air, then I came down to the ground.

He rushed forward to head-butt me and suddenly, everything

was in slow motion. As his head touched mine, I cracked his whole human body, and it crumbled away to reveal his non-dualistic form, which was like an immature child.

"Ah, there you are!" I said.

I felt compassion for him and revealed to the now glowing form of this man what he had become. The revelation of his essence self and the acknowledgment of how he had treated his son brought about a thorough transformation in his consciousness. I looked back at the son and saw that he was also healed, and I knew he'd be okay.

The Nightmare Rewrite Technique can be a powerful way of working with the Shadow in your dreams. Along with studying the Shadow in your dreams, you can use this technique to strengthen your ability to lucid-dream. Rather than looking at nightmares as something just there to trouble you, realize the profound potential for healing they hold. You are developing fearlessness in your dreamworld.

30

A Powerful Lucid Dream

It can be helpful to hear a grounded example of what these techniques look like in practice and how to utilize lucid dreaming for the healing of the psyche.

The following dream was a powerful turning point in Nisha's lucid-dreaming journey. It was the beginning of her devising the Nightmare Rewrite Technique. Although the material at the beginning of the dream was troubling, by sticking with the dream, instead of trying to flee from it, the healing of a deep existential fear took place.

NISHA'S Experience Leading up to the Nightmare Rewrite Technique

Towards the end of the year when I was having my encounter with a deep fear of death, I had a significant and profound lucid dream that changed the way I looked at everything. For me, the fear of death carried with it a questioning of this earthly reality in terms of "good versus evil." There was a paradox within humanity that my mind could not comprehend.

My question was this: "If the underlying source of creation and all things is loving and kind, then how can humans carry out such heinous and violent acts against each other?"

No matter how hard I thought about that question I could not reconcile the two thoughts. This led my mind to spiral into a dark place of wondering whether the core of the universe was actually love or chaos and violence. Unfortunately, this thought pattern leads us to see the Afterworld in dualistic terms of Heaven and Hell. I know and have seen the suffering of this earthly existence, but what if this doesn't end when we are released from our bodily form and, in fact, continues for eternity? These thoughts kept me up late into the night, physically shaking with fear. I needed confirmation that this idea was not real, yet my mind provided me with no solace.

Now that you understand the context and frame of mind in which this dream took place, let me tell you the dream:

The Nightmare that Brought This Fear Front and Center

I was traveling in Brazil with my Mom and a group of other people. We entered a building where they were carrying out an elaborate ritual. Everyone was dressed in white and sat up on the bleachers. We joined the people on the bleachers and looked down upon a dirt floor set up for the ceremony.

The room's atmosphere was heavy and grim, no one made eye contact with one another, and heads hung down as if in mourning. One by one people were called down to the center of the dirt floor room.

We watched as a handsome young man in his mid-twenties was called down. He walked over to a table with various ceremonial objects placed upon it. The young man scanned the table thoughtfully, carefully choosing which object to select. Finally, his eyes settled upon an ancient relic in the shape of a hook. It seemed to be carved out of bone.

He then took the hook object and suddenly plunged it into his chest, trying to scoop out his own heart.

I was absolutely terrified—so much so that I awoke from the dream in a panic. All of my fears about violence and humanity came crashing in like a tidal wave. I was trembling all over, and it felt like reality was closing in upon me.

Stumbling out of bed I went into my bathroom and stood in front of my reflection. My skin was gray, drained of all its color.

Still shaking I started a hot shower and sat under the warm waters attempting to calm myself.

During that time, I was reading Matt Kahn's book, *Whatever Arises, Love That*, so I attempted to open my heart to the terrifying dream vision. Over and over in my head, I repeated, "Love this dream, love this vision."

Eventually, I started to feel love wash over me along with the warm water from my shower. The fear was slowly giving way to love, and my trembling body began to calm. I turned off the shower and returned to bed.

Nightmare Rewrite of This Dream

Wrapping myself tightly in my down comforter, I settled into the warmth in my body and put all my attention on the pace of my breath. As I closed my eyes, I decided to keep holding the frequency of love within my mind while revisiting that terrifying image of the young man ripping out his heart.

Something entirely unexpected happened as I re-envisioned the dreamscape—I found myself fully slipping back into it, but this time I was lucid and aware that it was a dream.

The young man was in front of me on the floor, dead. Surrounding me, people were wailing in grief. I did not avert my eyes or try to escape or change the situation; instead, I kept watching the horrific scene in front of me.

To my shock, I began to see a blue figure emerging from the lifeless body of the young man. This figure floated out of his body like steam rising from a warm cup of tea until the humanoid blue figure was fully levitating outside the dead body.

He had no face or distinguishing features, but I could tell that it was the man who, just moments ago, was dead on the floor. Not using any words but with what felt like a tug to the center of my solar plexus, he urged me to follow him.

A simultaneous repulsion and attraction to follow him stirred within my body. Did I really want to see what he had in store for me next?

Nevertheless, amidst my apprehension, like a tiny spark igniting the flame of my inner knowing, I felt love. And so, I followed him. We started to both float up above the scene. I witnessed his body, the people mourning, and the terror of it all getting smaller and smaller as we were pulled up by an invisible force like helium balloons.

What happened next is hard to put into words, but I will try. We began moving through sections of color and tones. First a blue one, the same color as his amorphous body. All I could see was the blue hue and all I could hear was a singular tone. Then we moved into a purple hue, and his body changed to match the color of our surrounding landscape. The tone also changed.

Without words, he brought my attention to the fact that I no longer had a human body and yet could still hear with no ears and see with no eyes. I was baffled by this realization, but there was no time for my amazement, because we kept moving through colors and different tones—orange, then green, then yellow.

Finally, we came through to a pure white and the brightest tone yet. It was deafening, and I thought, "This is it, I am dead and consumed back into nothingness." This moment lasted for a moment beyond time.

To my surprise, however, it did come to an end. Out of the pure white began to appear shapes, bodies, and forms, both human and otherworldly. Everything was still quite bright, and it all felt like pure love and enjoyment.

Dragons flew around with gods and goddesses. It was a sight to see! Even in these forms, they didn't feel like the final form; more like an elaborate costume party where everyone got to pick their favorite form and change it at will. It was pure play! I truly enjoyed myself and spent quite a while around these beings.

Eventually, I felt another tug in my solar plexus, this time letting me know that it was fun to play like this, but I was tired of the perfection and still had much to experience and learn. With this tug, in lightning speed, I found myself diving back through all the tonal color bands and crashing into my body, jolting myself awake.

Laying back in my bed, cuddled up in my cozy down comforter I was awake and knew that I would never look at death in the same way again.

This was just the beginning of my adventures in lucid dreaming. I had yet to take on the study of *The Tibetan Book of the Dead* and Dream Yoga. When I did, I was shocked to realize that the layers of various colors and energy I had passed through in my lucid dream were very similar to the descriptions of the Six Worlds humans pass through after dying as outlined in *The Tibetan Book of the Dead*. Furthermore, the main purpose of Dream Yoga is to prepare for a lucid death. This is just one example of how dreams will tell you the path you are supposed to walk before your conscious awareness even knows it.

Advanced Lucid Dreaming Techniques

As you grow in your lucidity practice, you are cultivating a flexibility of mind that can translate into your daily life. By breaking the hold that recurring dreams and patterns have over you in your dreamworld, you are also diminishing the hold that habitual perceptions of the mind have over you in your waking life. You can literally see situations with new eyes.

Sometimes in dreams, you feel strong emotions, aversions, or attachments to what is going on, then once you become lucid you realize that it wasn't so serious after all and can be easily shifted. The empowerment and confidence that comes from that realization translate into the same realization about Ordinary Reality.

Most of the time, our suffering is rooted in the way we perceive the world. It is easy to know that yet hard to shift it. With lucid dreaming, you are practicing the skill of shifting your perception of dream reality at a moment's notice. Through lucid dreaming, you get a taste of the malleable nature of experience at first hand.

Within the path of Dream Yoga, one of the practices is to change the dream material at will. For example, in your lucid dream, try changing day into night and changing the environment around you in some way. You can also change your internal experience from sorrow to joy and anger to love. As Tenzin Wangyal Rinpoche says, "The purpose of these practices is to integrate lucidity and flexibility with every moment of life, and to let go of the heavily conditioned way we have of ordering reality, of making meaning, and of being trapped in delusion."

What follows are several things you can do to cultivate malleability of mind once you gain proficiency in lucid dreaming.

Multiply Objects in the Dream

Practicing increasing and decreasing the number of objects in a dream helps you see how you can shift situations in your waking life. For instance, if you are looking at one house, try and multiply it to a whole city of houses. If you feel that you lack something in an area of your life, increasing the number of objects within dreams strengthens the belief that life can be abundant. If you are feeling overwhelmed by too many things to take care of in your life, practicing decreasing objects in the dream helps show the psyche how it can remove unnecessary clutter from your life.

Shape-Shift

Change your physical form within the dream. Make yourself large or tiny, turn yourself into your power animal, change yourself into another gender or ethnicity, turn yourself into a tree. Shape-shifting has long been a skill of the mystic and shaman. Many Native American stories tell of the wise elder who was able to shape-shift in Ordinary Reality and walk in both worlds.

A Diné (Navajo) story from New Mexico tells of the shaman who told his students to watch as he walked down to the river. They watched carefully as he waded into the river up to his knees then disappeared. He had told them to go downriver a ways and wait for him there. They stood on that shore downriver for quite a while, watching and waiting, and finally, saw him emerge from the river and come toward them. Astonished, they asked where he had been, and he said that he had shape-shifted into a fish, swam downriver, and shape-shifted back to his human form.

From cultures as far apart as Greco-Roman mythology to Trinidadian folklore, shape-shifting has long been a skill acquired by high-level mystics. Practicing shape-shifting in your dreams enables your psyche to recognize the fluid and ever-changing nature of the Self. We often become stuck in specific Personas and patterns, clinging to them through overidentification. By changing our form in the Dreamtime, we learn to loosen the rigidity of the Self, becoming more adaptable in our sense of identity. This practice helps us shift and transform the Personas we've developed with greater ease. Just as you might journey into the Underworld through drumming, you can revisit a nightmare in your imagination after waking to heal what it has revealed—especially when the Persona you have reinforced becomes limiting or dysfunctional.

Another practice in the Dreamtime is to shape-shift into another person entirely. You can build a tremendous amount of empathy for the experiences of other humans by doing this practice. Occupying a body different from your own within a lucid dream feels incredibly real. This lucid way of taking a "walk in someone else's shoes" provides a great opportunity to see the world from a very different perspective.

Of course, this will not give you a full understanding of the lived experience of somebody from, say, another ethnicity who is in that body all the time and experiences oppression based on the body they were born into. However, you can utilize this practice to build more compassion and understanding for people who have different life experiences.

Change Your Emotional State

Emotions can be just as strong, if not more powerful, within a dream as opposed to waking reality. Have you ever had the experience in a dream of being incredibly angry about the most mundane thing? Or perhaps devastatingly sad over a minor inconvenience?

The Dreamtime is wonderful at highlighting how we really feel about situations we might be downplaying in waking reality. Experiencing a disproportionately strong emotional reaction to a situation can function as a dream sign. Next time you have an intense emotional reaction, use the "dream sign" to ask yourself if you could be dreaming and then do a state check. If it turns out that you were dreaming and you become lucid, practice changing your emotional state. When the realization that you were dreaming dawns on you, it is a relatively easy task to then shift the emotional state.

Recognizing that it is a dream, you are released from the spell and know that whatever you are reacting to isn't "real." Practice changing your emotions from anger to love, despair to joy, sadness to wonder. Shifting emotions in the dream will help you in waking reality, too. You come to realize that your emotional reactions, though valid, often become a habitual energetic pattern you fall into as the result of strongly held beliefs about yourself or other people. This way, you free yourself from overly reactive emotions.

That is not to say that you should suppress your emotions or "just be happy," if a situation is sad. Difficult emotions give us the energy and guidance to change something if situations are harmful. But they can become an addiction rather than guidance, and we may find ourselves getting high off certain negative emotions and becoming attached to that negative feedback loop. The practice of emotional state change is about breaking these dysfunctional patterns and recalibrating our emotions so that they don't have a harmful hold over our perception of reality.

Accomplish Supernatural Tasks

Within lucid dreams, you are freed from the limitations of waking reality. It can be extremely joyful and profound to do things you cannot do while awake, such as fly around, walk through walls, breathe underwater, travel to another galaxy, meet with interdimensional beings, and go to heavenly realms.

This practice has been discussed in relation to Upper World journeys. Engaging in the energies of Upper World journeys builds confidence and personal empowerment for your waking life. Waking up from a dream where you were stretched beyond the limitations of human form reminds you that you are more than this body. Consciousness expands beyond our single lifetime, and we are bigger than what is happening in our mundane reality.

Tapping into this realization you can appreciate the gift of a human life while not becoming overly trapped in the dramas of daily reality. A higher perspicacity can be achieved through this practice of performing supernatural tasks in the Dreamtime.

Fulfill Desires

Desire fulfillment is a common stage of progression with many lucid dreamers. Realizing that you can pretty much do whatever you want within a lucid dream is exciting indeed. Contrary to what one might think, fulfilling desires in the Dreamtime does not inherently mean that you will devolve into debauchery.

Recognizing desires inside your dreams can help you realize if you've been denying or suppressing things that truly make you happy in waking reality. Also, being able to experience the fulfillment of some desires in a lucid dream can actually sate that desire in waking reality and help you release attachment to the particular objects of desire.

Of course, you should work with a therapist if you struggle with addictive tendencies or the desires you are exploring are troubling, so that you can process these desires in the Dreamtime. For many, though, this stage of desire fulfillment can be extremely helpful. Once you've fulfilled many of your compelling desires in the dream realms, you can be released from them. Naturally, you then move on to wanting to have more transformational or healing experiences within a lucid dream.

Connect with Your Inner Guidance and Parts of Yourself

Another psychological task you can carry out in the lucid dream is connecting with various parts of yourself, from your inner child to your higher self. Ask those parts about what wounds from your past still need healing. Seek their guidance for daily dilemmas and big life choices. Tap into the wisdom that there is a part of you, your inner guidance system, which already knows the right answer.

This helps you become less dependent on external teachers or sources of knowledge. It is wonderful to find trusted guides; however, even while establishing a network of teachers, it is essential to learn to trust the inner teachers and wisdom that resides within you.

Meeting the Co-Author and Establishing the I–Thou Relationship Through Dreaming

When traveling in the lucid-dream realms, you quickly realize that your control over these realms has its limits. Mastery of the psyche in this context isn't about perfecting the manipulation of reality or the dreamscape, nor is it about dominating a psychedelic experience; rather, it is about entering into a conscious dialogue with your psyche and subconscious.

Through lucid dreaming, you experiment with your agency, or ability to create, and begin to realize that your control over these realms has its limitations. For example, you might change the sky from night to day, only for it to revert to night again unexpectedly, or you might create a field of flowers, only for them to transform into butterflies against your will and fly away. Such experiences are typical for lucid dreamers. While you have more influence over your dreams than usual, you are not in complete control. There is another force—be it your subconscious, higher self, or Spirit—collaborating with you in the lucid space.

We refer to this presence as the Co-Author, because it co-creates your lucid dreams with you. Encountering this "co-authoring" force can be a profoundly joyful experience, revealing a loving, caring presence within your psyche that is eager to connect with you.

Instead of you being the one in charge of these lucid states, you are being invited to engage in a conscious dialogue with your vast inner dimensions. By doing so, you establish what we have talked about previously, the "I–Thou" connection.

This presence that interacts with you playfully in lucid dreams is also a crucial part of the drum journey when you meet your spirit animal as an inner guide. Both modalities bring you into a relationship with the "Thou."

As you've learned, once you have established an awareness of this "I–Thou" relationship within, the relationship of the two, then you are much better prepared to engage with the third consciousness of the plant medicine. Having firmly established your inner guidance system through drumming journeys and lucid dreaming, you can trust yourself more fully within this relational inner cosmos.

Voyaging into the Dreamtime with lucidity, it is possible to work in harmony with the subconscious mind directly. In this relational exchange between the conscious and subconscious mind, we are building a bridge to form a more direct link into shadowy and blocked places within our psyche. Gently and steadily, in an organic way, we can work with the mind to loosen up and let go of falsely imposed limitations.

Ultimately, the goal is to integrate lucidity and flexibility into every moment of life. By continually challenging and transforming the apparent solidity of experiences and thoughts, we dissolve the conditioning that binds us. This practice then leads to a luminous and transparent understanding of reality, revealing the truth of the limitless freedom available in the mind.

You have developed the skills to navigate your mind through these practices, with your inner compass now finely tuned to guide you toward what areas of your psyche you're ready to explore and which to avoid. You've prepared yourself to confront the Shadow by journeying into the Underworld, facing it in nightmares, and engaging in challenging drumming experiences. With this solid foundation, you can now approach the realms of psychedelic consciousness with greater confidence.

PART 4

Psychedelics

32

Lucid Dreaming and Psychedelics

Since the early days of psychedelic therapy, people have approached the surprising contents of the psychedelic experience in a way analogous to how we approach dreams.
—MARC AIXALÀ, Psychedelic Integration

Now that you have learned about the powerful psychological, scientific, and spiritual benefits of lucid dreaming, you can begin to see how lucid dreaming serves as an excellent preparation for a psychedelic journey. Both lucid dreaming and psychedelic experiences involve altering the way the mind usually engages with reality. Through lucid dreaming you are altering how the mind works in the Dreamtime, growing new neuronal pathways, bringing it into a state of enhanced awareness. With psychedelics, you engage in a similar practice of expanding or altering your perception of reality beyond what you normally observe. Since both states of consciousness can share similar characteristics of heightened awareness, vivid imagery, and profound insights, we can view a psychedelic journey as the Dreamtime coming into Ordinary Reality. Gaining more expertise in working with the Dreamtime before ingesting an entheogen helps prepare you to engage with the psychedelic state of consciousness.

The practice of lucid dreaming requires a great deal of disciplined awareness and mindfulness. It strengthens the practice of being very present in waking reality by requiring you to regularly perform state checks. By asking yourself if you could be dreaming, you bring yourself into a heightened mindfulness in your waking state. Much like a meditation practice, it puts you in touch with your sensory awareness, your embodied presence. You are not dissociated but very aware of what your body is feeling/sensing in Ordinary Reality.

Then within the dream state, practicing lucid dreaming requires that you maintain a high state of awareness so that you don't slip back into a non-lucid dream. By practicing these skills through lucid dreaming, you can increase your overall ability to stay present moment by moment, which is crucial during a psychedelic journey. In this way, you will be better prepared to navigate the often intense and unpredictable nature of psychedelic experiences.

How Lucid Dreaming Helps with Psychedelic Journeys

Calling on Your Allies

If you feel overwhelmed by emotional states, recall your practices of shifting emotions in the lucid dream journeys you've gone on. Remember to call on your allies to help you, both the physical ones in Ordinary Reality and the energetic ones with whom you have developed a relationship in your drumming and dreaming journeys.

Shape-Shifting

Oftentimes, the body can feel uncomfortable at certain points of the psychedelic journey. When this is the case, remember your lucid dreaming work with shape-shifting. Come into your body in a new way. Let it move like your power animal and shake off the uncomfortable feelings. Follow the feelings without resisting them, allowing a melting feeling to wash over your body, or give in to visualizations of the person next to you looking like a deer with antlers. There is much to learn from the particular sensations and visions that come to you. If you recall that your body can take many forms, you can follow the feeling of extreme expansion or contraction with less anxiety. In your dreams, you have played around with being all shapes and sizes, so this feeling is no longer foreign. When your body is feeling especially overwhelmed, breathe into your lucid awareness, and acknowledge what state you are in (a psychedelic-altered one). Just as a dream passes, this too will pass.

Recall Your Clear Intent

While on the ride the psychedelics are taking you on, your task is to remain grounded in lucidity. Just as within a lucid dream, this grounding comes from your Intent. Come back to the "why" of why you choose to ingest the substances in the first place. When you take on this practice, even challenging or hard journeys do not need to be looked at as "bad trips." Everything that happens has a message that you have invoked.

Practice Having Agency

Notice the shadows that are coming up, just as you would in a lucid nightmare, and be willing to deal with them with lucidity. Remember how you were able to face and transform fears in your dreams. Try working with the techniques outlined in Chapter 29 (page 184) to better cope with fears and anxieties that arise in the psychedelic journey.

Through lucid dreaming, you can become more comfortable with exploring your inner thoughts and emotions. This is a key component of psychedelic experiences. You've learned how to gain some sense of agency within your experiences in lucid dreams. By knowing how to navigate your dream environments with agency, you can have better agency during a psychedelic journey.

Know Your Symbol System

Both lucid dreams and psychedelic experiences often feature rich symbolism and archetypal imagery. When you have studied the unique language of symbols and metaphors from your dreams speak through, you can better understand and interpret the symbolic content of your psychedelic experiences. Look back at your dream journal before entering a psychedelic journey to remind yourself of your personal dream symbols and metaphors.

A spontaneous "aha" moment may arise, when you see the symbols from your dream coming into the psychedelic journey. You will no longer be dependent on others to interpret them for you or confused by what they represent. When you become deeply familiar with your personal symbolic meanings and patterns, it's like learning to understand a new language – but one that comes from within yourself. You start to recognize and interpret the unique ways your unconscious mind communicates through dreams, feelings, and intuitions. Once you develop this inner fluency, you can have meaningful dialogues with parts of yourself that operate beyond ordinary conscious thought. This deeper self-understanding gives you valuable insights and a greater sense of wholeness. This is a truly empowering achievement.

Integration and Reflection

Just as you take time each morning to integrate and write down your lucid dreaming experiences, this reflective practice is also crucial for integrating psychedelic experiences. Write about your psychedelic journey after you've come back into Ordinary Reality. You can even format your psychedelic reflections in a similar way as in your dream journal:

- Give your journey a title to help summarize the overall experience.
- Write down the journey in its entirety to capture the full experience.
- Note any particularly strong emotions as well as the overall emotional content of the journey.
- Highlight "dream signs" that came into your psychedelic journey.
- Note when you performed "state checks" and how they helped you ground into the reality you were experiencing.
- Take care to recognize the crossovers and synchronicities between dreams leading up to the journey and the journey itself. Similarly, note what was going on in your Ordinary Reality that influenced or came into your psychedelic journey.
- Note what levels of lucidity you went through during your journey. Were there moments when you were non-lucid, semi-lucid, or fully lucid? What did that look like for you on a psychedelic journey?

Once you've taken the time to do your personal reflection, share your insights with trusted allies. This helps to ground it back in your Ordinary Reality. This will help you make meaning of the psychedelic journey you just went on. "Making meaning" is a core element of being able to process and make use of your journey.

Dreamwork and Psychedelic Practices Across Cultures

Many cultures view dreamwork and psychedelic practices as complementary, using them together to gain a deeper understanding of the mind, spirit, and collective well-being. Historically, cultures have used dreamwork and psychedelic practices in tandem to enhance personal and communal well-being.

Aboriginal Australian cultures place a strong emphasis on the Dreamtime, the foundational epoch of creation. The psychoactive plant pituri is cited to have been used by them to assist with stamina and help induce trance states. The Dreamtime, or "The Dreaming," as they call it, is central to the spiritual and cultural life of Aboriginal Australian people. This concept encompasses the creation period when ancestral beings shaped the world, as well as an ongoing, timeless reality that connects the past, present, and future.

Dreamwork within this framework is not only a means of personal insight but also a way to maintain cultural continuity, spiritual well-being, and connection to the land.

The Dreamtime refers to the period when ancestral beings created the landscape, established laws, and instituted cultural practices. Unlike linear Western conceptions of time, Dreamtime is cyclical and ever-present. It embraces the past, present, and future. It is an eternal moment that Australian Aboriginal people access through rituals, stories, and dreams, allowing them to connect with the ancestral past and the spiritual essence of the world. Furthermore, the landscape is imbued with the presence of ancestral beings, making the land itself a living part of the Dreaming.

Elders and shamans often interpret dreams to provide insight and advice, understanding the symbolic language of the Dreaming. All the people regularly practice dream-sharing within the community which helps reinforce cultural values and collective knowledge. Dreams can reveal the causes of illness and the necessary instructions for healing that the community then undertakes. Shamans and elders hold a pivotal role in facilitating access to the Dreaming. They are highly respected as possessing deep knowledge of the spiritual world and the ability to navigate between realms, often guiding others in their dream journeys.

NORMA'S Studies of Aboriginal Tracking Skills

I studied for several years in the high desert of New Mexico with John Stokes, who lived in the Australian Outback with Aboriginal people for over 10 years in the 1970s and 1980s. He taught us many skills key to surviving in the harsh desert setting— animal tracking, ways of making fire, plant identification, and foraging. Learning all of these practical skills required that we slow way down and hone our attunement to the environment. He had us notice the way a tree branch was bent from a deer passing by, or where a few pebbles were turned over by the swift push of a coyote's paw. We had to become hyperaware of Ordinary Reality in order to be aware in the Dreamtime. Tracking has to be mastered both in Ordinary Reality and the Dreamtime.

Ancient European cultures. The excellent research done by Brian Muraresku and published in *The Immortality Key: The Secret History of the Religion with No Name* has brought to light that rich traditions of dream interpretation and use of psychoactive substances existed in ancient European cultures. These practices were integral to their spiritual, healing, and philosophical explorations.

One of the most famous examples of psychedelic use was in the Eleusinian Mysteries in Ancient Greece, a series of initiation ceremonies held in honor of the mother and daughter goddesses Demeter and Persephone. These rites were conducted annually for nearly 2,000 years and are believed to have included the consumption of a psychoactive potion known as kykeon. This drink, likely containing ergot, a fungus that grows on barley that is a natural source of LSD-like compounds, induced altered states of consciousness that allowed initiates to experience profound spiritual visions. Participants often experienced vivid dreams and visions during the ceremonies, which were interpreted as divine messages and transformative spiritual experiences.

Ancient Greeks placed importance on dreams in the context of healing and divination. The practice of incubation, or sleeping in sacred spaces to receive healing dreams, was central to the cult of Asclepius, the god of medicine. The dreams they had while in these sacred spaces were interpreted by priests and priestesses, who provided guidance and remedies based on the dream content. Furthermore, oracles, such as the Oracle of Delphi, may have reached altered states induced by natural gases at that sacred site, which gave them the visions to deliver their prophecies.

Bacchanalia, the ancient Roman counterpart to the Dionysian rites of the Greek, were ecstatic festivals in honor of Bacchus, the god of wine, freedom, intoxication, and ecstasy. These rites involved the use of wine and possibly other intoxicants to achieve states of altered consciousness. Like the Greeks, Romans believed in the power of dreams to convey messages from the gods. They often sought interpretations from seers and priests. Dreams were a major source of divinatory insight, with professional dream interpreters (oneiromancers) playing a significant role in Roman society.

The Celtic and Druid traditions of ancient Europe also have a rich history of using dreams and psychoactive substances for spiritual and healing purposes. While the historical evidence is less abundant than for the ancient Greeks and Romans, there are significant indications that these practices were integral to Celtic and Druid spirituality. Some scholars believe that the red-capped mushroom, *Amanita muscaria*, known for its psychoactive properties, was used by Druids in rituals.

This mushroom grows in the regions historically inhabited by the Celts. In his book *The Shamanic Way of the Bee: Ancient Wisdom and Healing Practices of the Bee Masters,* Simon Buxton uncovers an ancient Celtic mystery school practice of inducing altered states in the initiates through a series of bee stings.

As we have discussed earlier, dreams played a significant role in Celtic spirituality, often seen as messages from the Otherworld, a mystical realm inhabited by deities, spirits, and ancestors. The Celts believed that dreams could provide important guidance, prophecy, and healing. Sacred sites such as wells, groves, and burial mounds were used for incubation of the dreams. Sacred groves of trees, known as nemetons, were central to Druidic rituals. Beyond psychedelic ingestion, there are many accounts of Druids entering ecstatic states during rituals facilitated by rhythmic drumming and chanting. These altered states induced by drumming were used for communication with the divine and accessing these Dreamtime realms.

There is great wisdom in recognizing that many cultures have combined the power of dreaming with the use of psychoactive substances to engage with the psyche.

As you begin to explore the conscious and intentional use of psychedelic substances, it's important to dedicate plenty of time to connecting with your dream world. This is our core teaching – that it is not merely an option but a necessity to track the maps of your own psyche with the tools you learn in shamanic drumming trance states and dreaming techniques. Then you will better comprehend the symbol systems and navigate your psyche to the accurate information that your unconscious is longing to share with you.

33

The Rhythm of a Psychedelic Journey

When you train with the Huichol, you realize that there is a rhythm to the process of working with psychedelics. It is not random. In Huichol and other Indigenous ceremonies there is a commonality of experience, a flow of when to go within and when to focus externally, as natural as breathing in and out. In a ceremony as intricate as a choreographed dance, the guides are tuned into the collective experience and facilitate when to slow down and when to move more quickly, when to sit and when to dance and shake.

As we go through the stages in this chapter, you will notice this rhythm playing out. In medieval Western mysticism, this rhythm of the journey back and forth between inner and outer is called *apophatic* (expansion) and *cataphatic* (contraction). This ability to expand, contract, and oscillate between expansion and contraction is a key to trauma healing.

Oftentimes within psychedelic journeys, people will encounter the natural expansion and contraction that happens in altered consciousness. Without proper guidance this can be overwhelming, because perceptual reality actually expands into visions of everything everywhere all at once, then contracts into the void or nothingness. Learning how to trust and ride the waves of this expansion and contraction relieves anxiety when working with plant medicines. In his trauma healing work, biologist Peter Levine, developer of Somatic Experiencing™, calls this the necessity of *pendulating* between the wound and the relief.

When working with deep traumas it's important to not just stay in the trauma experience. The body, mind, and soul need to *regulate* themselves through the practice of going into the hurt places and then back out into grounding and nurturing experiences. By doing this you avoid overstimulation and re-traumatization.

Oftentimes our culture can fixate on getting things done as quickly as possible and "pushing through" to the other side. Trauma wounds can be brought to the surface too rapidly and before the scaffolding of the personality is ready to bear the weight of these revelations. This can lead to a person becoming very frightened and result in further fragmentation of the mind rather than integration. At times, such improper force applied to the psyche can even lead to an overwhelming shame, suicidal ideation, and a collapse of self-esteem. Pointing out and identifying the trauma is one thing, but actually having the skill and right timing to bring about healing is another magnitude of adept mastery.

As Marc Aixalà says in *Psychedelic Integration*:

> Issues such as life and death; coming face to face with insanity and the fear of losing control; intense emotions of anger, fear, or sadness; and spiritual revelations and ecstatic experiences are all elements that frequently appear in psychedelic experiences . . . although we each have our particular and individual phenomenological manifestations, the individual process and the collective process run in parallel.

Along with personal traumas, collective existential worries often come into play when entering into an altered space through psychedelics. Knowing that these issues are part of the collective unconscious and are common directions for the psyche to explore can be helpful. You are not alone in the fears and emotions you are facing.

As with drumming journeys and lucid dreaming, by studying the shadows and fears present within your waking reality you are better prepared to anticipate what configuration the Shadow will take in your plant medicine journey.

By following a path that allows a gentle progression through various states of altered consciousness—from drumming to lucid dreaming—you can slowly unravel the Shadow and heal traumas more adequately; the shadows that arise within plant medicine journeys will then be familiar and more manageable. If you are looking for a breakthrough within a psychedelic journey, having a map of conscious exploration into the altered mind will help you achieve that. The rhythm and framework provide guidance on how to walk in and out of a psychedelic journey in a more structured way and find the epiphany moments.

One of the main purposes of venturing into alternative states of consciousness through plant medicine journeys is to gain more freedom from stuck perceptions. As we have been exploring, in most cases what binds the mind with the tightest ropes is how trapped we can become in our conditioned personality.

To counter the habituated self, one must be present on three levels: the physical, energetic, and subconscious. Through this act of heightened awareness (lucidity), you are called to the impeccable use of energy. It is helpful to interrupt the patterns of numbing out, dissociating, or denying so that you can arrive at more conscious awareness.

Another shield many people put up during psychedelic experiences is one of self-importance and holding judgments of others. This pathway requires that you ground yourself and open your heart. Surrendering to the plant medicines requires a great deal of humility, because they can strip away your outer protective layers—allow the pain to be felt and grace to flow through you in order to transmute the energies.

For a lasting pattern shift, this deep Shadow integration practice must be nurtured over time, practiced diligently, and integrated into your life. It may sound like a lot of work, but the reward is a lasting freedom from habitual patterns that before felt impossible to change.

In doing this work within our innermost selves we become the alchemists of our souls. As such, we create the inner union—the *hieros gamos*, or marriage of Heaven and Earth—within our very being. We become the unifying bridge between the dimensions of waking reality and the dream realms. Alchemists call this inner union the Great Work.

34

Preparing for the Journey —
Art-Making, Self-Screening, Threshold Guardians

For our Huichol teachers, art serves to express one's personal subconscious imagery, while also keeping in close relationship with the power of these ancient archetypal symbols. As you explore and catalog the symbolism within your psyche through drumming journeys and lucid dreaming, you may encounter the challenge of expressing these experiences solely through words.

Language often falls short in conveying the depth of symbolic content found in dreams. Since dreams communicate through rich symbols, adequately describing them can be difficult. Incorporating artistic and visual expressions to represent these metaphors can provide a valuable means of communicating and translating the messages conveyed by your dreams.

Art-Making as Preparation for Psychedelic Journeys

Making art from your drumming journeys and dreams can be extremely enlightening. This can include various forms, such as paintings, collages, or dance pieces. Creating art allows the nonverbal aspects of yourself to express and channel the energies emerging from your subconscious.

Before embarking on a psychedelic journey, review the art generated from your previous explorations to help set the tone for your upcoming experience. Additionally, take time to create art that reflects the Intention you have for this particular journey. This artistic snapshot of your goals for the psychedelic experience can aid in making sense of it once you have emerged out on the other side.

Within wisdom traditions, art is not just about the individual isolated in a specific place in time, but is rather intimately interwoven with the images of the ancestral lineage. Huichol men, women, and children spend much of their time creating works of art that reflect their unique cosmology. They embroider images from their Dreamtime realms on their clothing: deer, birds, and other animals; flowers; plant medicine; and symbols for the sun, moon, earth, fire, and water. Their unique way of representing these beings and elements in geometric patterns goes back to ancient times and is a language in and of itself.

Making these works of art also strengthens the bond with the *codified identity* of one's cultural mythology. In the Huichol teachings, taking the time to make this intricate art focuses their intention on connecting with particular animals and elemental deities, and on receiving messages from them.

Fig. 12: *A God's Eye, or Ojo de Dios, from Quemado Mountain, San Luis Potosi, Mexico* (photo by Anaroza)

Before a plant medicine journey, we were always instructed to create God's eye yarn weavings and prayer arrow art pieces. During the creation of these art forms, we spent many hours mulling over our Intention for the upcoming journey and getting clearer on what we were called to grapple with in the Underworld of our psyche. After making these precious works of art, we sent them as prayers to the other dimensions—first, by taking great care in making them very beautiful and then, by releasing them in ceremonies of burying or burning them before we partook of the plant medicine.

NORMA'S Experience Making the Prayer Arrow and Letting Go

The first time I created an elaborate prayer arrow with my teacher, Grandmother Guadalupe, it had such a powerful impact on me. She did not tell us beforehand that we would be burying the prayer arrows, and we spent a whole day carefully creating these works of beauty, which we were so proud of and became quite attached to.

It came as a shock when she announced that we would be burying them. A powerful lesson in letting go and non-attachment, we had to lay our prayer arrows in a deep hole in the earth and bury these precious, carefully crafted artworks before we went into the ceremony.

As I laid mine into the earth, I felt the grief of having to let go of something I had spent so much time on and cared about. This is the grief we all must face in the days, months, and years of our lives as we learn that part of being alive is having to let go of things we care for deeply. Ultimately, we will have to let go of our most precious possession, our human body, when we face our death. In the plant medicine journey, in order to receive its gift, a shedding of our previously held identity would be required.

After peyote journeys, the Huichol individually express what comes from their altered-state journeys by making more art.

Fig. 13: Cuadro de Estambre (Nierikas): Arte del Pueblo Wixárika (Huichol). Artwork by Juan Carlos Fonseca Mata.

Creating beautiful artwork is a core aspect of both preparing for and integrating plant medicine journeys in Huichol culture. Art is not a frivolous thing but rather, an essential aspect of the journey. Through doing the intricate, focused hand-work, the Huichol people are making the utmost effort to focus their minds and hearts on creating Beauty. Through the act of accepting all experiences as gifts, not labeling them as a good or bad trip, and then making art from that experience, they are alchemically transmuting the negative into the positive.

The Diné (Navajo) have a similar outlook on the need to link art and altered-state journeys. A core Diné teaching is about walking in The Beauty Way (the Navajo word *hozho* means "the beauty way," which implies a non-dual spiritual outlook in which everything is connected and influences everything else). In prayers of Intent, they call out to Beauty and proclaim that "Beauty is behind me, Beauty is before me, Beauty is above and below me." To find beauty is the Intention that is set with strong determination. Through this focus on creating beauty, any situation encountered, no matter how challenging it is, can come through to a creative solution or non-dualistic outcome. Finding the beauty in every experience is a deep training of your psyche to put on a different lens that radically shifts your perception.

Screening Yourself for the Psychedelic Journey

It's important to assess if you are really ready to embark on a plant medicine journey. Similarly, if you are facilitating a journey for someone else, you should also consider if they are truly ready. Don't move forward with it just because your ego persuades you or another person is pressuring you.

Initial Questions to Assess Readiness for the Journey

You want to evaluate if you are ready to undertake the transformational process of this journey on several different levels: Body, Mind, Spirit, Relationships, and Environment. The time of contemplation can be hours, days, weeks, or even years. Importantly, during this time you (or the person you are guiding) will be watching for signs which will appear in one's daily life or nighttime dreams. These signs will be clear indications if and when the plant medicine journey should take place.

Use the Journey to Completion Map to remind yourself about Affirmations and Threshold Guardians in relation to screening for the psychedelic experience:

- **Affirmations** are positive signs that arrive like passing messengers. You might come across a book or something online that seems to speak directly to your quest. Or a repetitive dream might be speaking to you in the language of symbols about your readiness to embark on a plant medicine journey. In short, the affirmations let you know that you are on the right path and that it is a good time for you to traverse the far reaches of your psyche and receive its gift with the assistance of plant medicines.

- **Threshold Guardians** are things that might come along to block you from doing the plant medicine journey, either outer obstacles or inner blockages. Some examples of Threshold Guardians are losing your car keys before coming to the session, a high level of fear or distrust that feels insurmountable, a guide who has to reschedule or cancel last minute, or becoming sick right before your journey.

These obstacles arise because Spirit wants you to fully commit to the journey of deconstructing your identity, rather than abandoning it midway. Once you enter the Underworld, it is crucial to traverse it completely and return with a meaningful gift or insight. Similar to drumming journeys, you should be able to retrace your steps and exit through the same portal you entered, ritually closing this sacred entry point. This practice ensures that you reclaim all the insights and aspects of yourself from the experience. Failing to do so might necessitate another journey, solely to retrieve what was left behind previously.

In essence, a "bad trip" can be one in which parts of yourself were left in the Underworld because the journey you went on was too intense. This can result in carrying a load of unmetabolized shadow material forward into your life. The path is one of the deconstruction or dismemberment of the ego and eventual integration or reconstruction, so it's better to pause at the threshold and consider at the start if you have the determination and resourcing to make it through or not.

Even if the roadblocks or delays that present themselves seem negative or frustrating at the time, they are actually protecting you. They give you a moment to question if you are ready and feel safe enough to deal with your Shadow material in the plant medicine journey.

Journal about any Threshold Guardians that are arising and any questions you have about your preparedness for the journey. At the same time, journal about the Affirmations you've received for the particular journey you are contemplating.

Once you are sure that you are ready to cross the Threshold Guardians and continue this journey you will prepare yourself for it.

35

Setting Your Intent for the Psychedelic Journey

Plant medicines can be disorienting because they bring the Dreamtime into Ordinary Reality. This is why the Huichol have us step over a ritual line into the psychedelic Dreamtime, so that we make a conscious note of the fact that we are entering a new realm of perception. As we do this ritual act, we name three things—what we are leaving, where we are going, and where we will return to:

- **You are leaving** Ordinary Reality and the persistent wash of perceiving all that surrounds you. "Leaving some skin at the doorway" means that you are required to let go of something significant that has been holding you back.
- **You are going** into non-Ordinary Reality, the liminal, the unknown. You will dwell there for a time and meet the challenges that await you in that space. If you have adequately prepared yourself, you will receive great personal gifts for having undertaken the journey.
- **You will return to** Ordinary Reality; however, if you were able to integrate what you experienced on the journey, the reality you left will not be the same, because you have changed. This is because you have regained some of your power, so the structures of Ordinary Reality will reconfigure to adjust to who you have become.

Once the journey we are about to embark on has been acknowledged, Indigenous elders would always have us prepare for this voyage physically and mentally.

Physical Preparation

Physical preparation can include: following a specific healthy diet and refraining (fasting) from alcohol, drugs, sex, as well as donning special clothing, and being well rested. These cleansing rituals are called *limpias* (cleansing) and *chupas* (extractions) in Mazatec language.

Culturally, Huichol preparation may look different from the preparation you might do. However, it is a good idea to cleanse your body beforehand in some manner, so it is prepared to ingest the altering substances. One of the purposes of refraining (fasting) from various substances and activities is to release attachments to conditioned desires. Becoming overly attached to certain substances and activities can create major distractions from your Intent while on the journey. Taking enough time to release the "grip" of these things is a helpful way to prevent too many distractions while in the altered state.

Selecting Your Starting Place and Formulating Your Intent

The environment in which you decide to ingest the plant medicine is your portal from one world into the other. Therefore, selecting and setting up this portal entry place as carefully as you would for your drumming journey is of utmost importance. The Huichol take great care of their portal entry place, or *nierika*, knowing how much power it holds in their own psyche.

While the Huichol use peyote, you can receive help selecting which psychoactive substance is best for you and discern the type of journey you'd like to have. Although the particular effects of each psychedelic will be different, the general rhythm remains the same. It may just be more or less obvious, especially if you are not used to tracking this rhythm. **With time, you will learn to follow this rhythm in various psychedelic journeys, regardless of the substance used to achieve the altered state.** By setting a clear and strong Intent, the traveler of the psyche will not enter in a haphazard way but rather, with a clear mission and purpose. This action, in and of itself, will greatly help in steering you away from fragmenting experiences. Even if you encounter challenging situations (which you often do when working with plant medicines), you can see the bigger picture of how it all is working together to help you accomplish your Intent.

Having a clear Intent helps anchor your mind around meaning-making. By orienting the mind in this way you give it purpose, just like the use of digging to focus the mind through the tunnel phase in the drumming journeys. The mind will be looking for clues and signs as to what part of your Intent the journey is helping you accomplish.

In the Huichol tradition, before ingesting the medicine, each person vocalizes their *Intent statement* for the group to witness. If you are working with a group, hearing one another's prayers begins to create a sense of community, trust, and bonding in the shared moment. Bringing everyone's Intent into the circle creates its own collective field, and you become allies with one another in accomplishing your Intent. If you are going on a journey by yourself or just with a guide, setting your Intent is still important. Write it down and then read it out loud to yourself or to your guide.

Questions for setting your Intent include:

- **Via Positiva:** What is the next stage of power you are being called to undertake? Does it relate to your work life, your intimate relationship life? Does it involve changing some core behavior pattern so that you are able to receive a new blessing? Do you want to have courage to be able to take action so that you can move into some new career, or new adventure of travel?
- **Via Negativa:** What traumas and shadows are you willing to explore in order to accomplish this Intent? How are those shadows related to what you are hoping to achieve? How do they hold you back from your next stage of growth?

Hand-write your Intent statement, including the two components of the Calling: the positive heart's desires you have for your future good and change in perspective, as well as the Shadow elements you are willing to examine and receive gifts from as a result of the plant medicine journey.

It might be scary to look at the shadows and traumas when setting your Intent, but it is crucial. They can arise whether or not you want to face them, so by honestly addressing them beforehand you are preparing yourself for what lies ahead. Going into the journey informed and ready for what can come up allows you to feel empowered.

It is also the perfect opportunity to honestly question one more time if you are ready to undertake this profound journey. This moment can serve as a final Threshold Guardian questioning if the traumas feel too big or scary for you to face. If this is the case, it might not be the right time to go into a plant medicine journey.

In the non-ordinary states of consciousness, you are even more affected by the fears that surround your trauma wounds. The best thing to do is to work with a Shadow work expert and therapist to deal with your traumas in waking life first. Get to a point where you feel that they are healed enough and then you will be ready to take them to an even deeper level of healing in the psychedelic experience.

Ritual at the Threshold

As with lucid dreaming and drumming journeys, you can take on the ritual practice of drawing a tarot or oracle card before ingesting the plant medicine. Through this divination, you can gain even clearer insight into what you may encounter on the journey. Try pulling a card for the Intent of what you hope to accomplish and another card for what shadows you may need to face in order to do so. This practice can set a profound tone for the journey.

The moment of ingesting the plant medicine is also important. Think of it as taking a step through the doorway of reality, out of the known and into the great mystery. With the Huichol, we approached the altar and drank the peyote in a liquid brew in front of Guadalupe. The dosage used was extreme, so we had to deeply trust our guide, trust that we were doing the right thing, and trust that we would make it back safely and the better for having gone through this.

That is why the preparation beforehand was so rigorous, because if we weren't ready, we would be getting in over our heads. It was essential to have our trustworthy guide at the steps of the portal, as she helped us feel trust in the trip we were about to undertake.

Now that it is legal to use psychedelic-assisted therapy in Oregon and Colorado (and other states will probably soon follow suit), it has become a more accessible way of gaining entry into altered states. Different substances have different strengths. When deciding upon your psychedelic (psilocybin and ketamine are the main ones legally available currently) and the facilitator who will be guiding you, think about the type of journey you want to go on.

Make sure that the guide you are working with is skilled in that particular medicine and that dosages have been pretested with the exact compound you are taking.

Grandmother Guadalupe repeated over and over to us to "trust the medicine." "Trusting the medicine" means that you will have the exact journey you are supposed to have, regardless of the dose or strength. Try not to enter into the journey with too many expectations of how it "should be." In essence, you are setting your Intent, which is the *why* of your trip, then surrendering to whatever the consciousness of the plant deems necessary for your growth.

The way I was taught, the guide takes the medicine too. Usually, the shaman takes the same dose or more. However, this is not the way many clinical groups or facilitation programs teach it. Use your discretion when it comes to your guide taking the medicine or not. It depends on the guide's lineage as well as skill in navigating the altered states.

Following this ancient well-trodden pathway, having formulated a clear Intent and stepped over the line with the proper rituals into the altered state, the voyager will enter the psychedelic Dreamtime with a true ability to trust the medicine.

36

Entering the Psychedelic Dreamtime

It can be a gradual process or a quick shift. Either way, the lines between Ordinary Reality and the Dreamtime begin to blur once you've ingested the psychedelic.

During this time of the initial onset, you are in a liminal space. Liminal space is what Celtic mystics called "betwixt and between." You are letting go of one state of consciousness and not all the way to where you are going. Remember the training you've received thus far on how to stay conscious when in liminal spaces.

Just as with the practice of crossing over into a drumming journey or lucid dreaming state, focusing your mind on your Intent will help you maintain lucidity as the world around you begins to deconstruct and shape-shift. You may experience unusual feelings as the medicine begins to take hold. It's common to feel swirling and twisting sensations. Interestingly, these sensations are similar to ones that can sometimes accompany an Out of Body Experience (OBE).

The unusual sensations associated with letting go can be physical, such as "my body is melting," or mental/emotional, such as "Am I going crazy? Am I losing my mind?" Some people feel as if they are dying. If you have a guide with you on your journey, you can let them know that you want reassurance. If you are by yourself, make sure to soothe yourself and affirm that this is the experience of your identity deconstructing and that your body is actually fine.

With our Huichol teachers, when anyone was having an especially hard time during this phase, the assistants to the shaman might ask to hold and gently massage the feet of the struggling voyager. By anchoring the voyager back into their bodies and bringing attention to the feet, they assisted in helping the intense feelings move out through the feet. If you are being a guide for others, take note, as these uncomfortable physical and psychological effects do arise. In such a case, some voyagers may want to keep arranging their space or even continue to move around the room and converse normally. These can all be ways of trying to ease the discomfort. Assist them in finding a space and position in which they can feel the most comfortable and help them relax into their bodies. Sometimes the discomfort in the body can even relate to the Shadow that is arising to be dealt with more deeply in the journey.

> **NORMA'S** Example of Helping a Client at This Stage
>
> On one occasion when a participant was very fidgety and discontent with the music choices, he asked to leave the room, so I went with him and left my assistant with the others. I helped him process what was coming up for him. It turned out that he was feeling a lot of anger that his father had died when he was young and realized that he had a Shadow habit pattern of being very critical of his environment, constantly trying to rearrange things to make himself feel less vulnerable to what had been so utterly uncontrollable. When he made this connection, it helped him relax into the process and genuinely feel more at ease, thus, he was able to join the group again feeling grounded and content.

At this stage, if you or someone you are guiding are encountering difficulties, then doing a drumming journey can also be beneficial. We recommend this with the caveat that the initial onset phase of some entheogens is slow enough to allow for the focus, while others may have a very quick onset and the focus to participate in a drum journey is not possible.

This drum journey can help the voyager connect with the symbolic realm and find meaning in the messages emerging from their Threshold Guardians or defense mechanisms. As previously discussed, drumming journeys allow travelers to delve deeply into their psyches and access their inner guidance systems. When in an altered state induced by psychedelics, drumming journeys become even more potent, as the symbolic world more readily intersects with Ordinary Reality.

Going on a drumming journey will connect you with your power animal, which immediately helps anchor you in the inner guidance system you've been cultivating for yourself. The reassurance of making it through the tunnel by digging and then connecting with the power animal, one's familiar inner guide, can be very comforting. Follow your power animal closely, and see what it wants to show you about being in this altered space. Make sure not to skip the step of coming back out the exact way you went in by retracing your steps. By engaging in this practice while in an already altered state, you are sharpening your mind's focus and accessing the symbolic realms in an organized way.

> **NORMA'S** Example of Helping a Voyager at This Stage
>
> For example, one voyager had no awareness of the state shift after she ingested the psychedelics and was struggling to enter into an altered state. Her mind's grip on ordinary consciousness was strong. I performed a drumming journey for her, and almost immediately she had a vivid visitation by an alligator power animal. It taught her many things about the degree of protection she needed in order to trust the experience. Once she connected with this strong ally, it helped her release her fears and resistance, and she had a powerful experience.

The Core of the Psychedelic Dreamtime

Once you are about midway into the process you are entering the core of the psychedelic Dreamtime. For some people, this can begin with an easy, ecstatic period; for example, seeing amazing geometric castles of gold, beautiful fractal patterns, or a heightened illumination of your surroundings.

However, for others, it can be disorienting and disturbing. At some moments you may be confused by the content or the intensity of the visions. It can feel as if you are being overcome by the medicine and carried by the experience, instead of being in control. Overwhelming fluctuations of sensory feelings of melting or flashing color grids flood your psyche regardless of whether your eyes are open or closed.

One of the keys when facing the more intense psychedelic sensations is to remain in a place of surrender. If you can let go of fears, expectations, and concerns about personal identity, you will save yourself from a stressful journey. Rather than trying to contract or restrict the experience, be open to experiencing other dimensions of reality. Approach it with a playful curiosity, even when it is challenging. You made the conscious choice to venture out of Ordinary Reality into the unknown, so don't let the mind trick you into wishing for things to be different from what they are.

Reconnect with your Intent statement again in these challenging moments. Remember what you are here to "know" and the shadows you must face in order to do so. All of the work you've done with lucid dreaming will be of great assistance at this stage. Recall the levels of personal empowerment you reached through facing your fears and nightmares. Through diligently working with the Dreamtime, you develop the ability to work with the material the psyche presents, even when it is hard.

When you release the need for control over the experience the "knowing," the *gnosis*, can begin to take place. Gnosis is a "direct knowing" through a lucid, sensory interaction with altered consciousness. This is a time to move past resistance and into accepting what is given to be felt and known; that is why it's called the stage of opening and letting go into the experience that is being given to you.

This is also a great moment to study the Shadow. In the next chapter, we will elaborate on how to study the Shadow throughout the psychedelic journey. For now, remember the Outer/Inner chart of the Journey to Completion methodology for sequestering the Shadow as it arises.

Within the psychedelic journey, the Shadow can present itself through others in the room; for example, your own guide may become your Outer Shadow, as can other participants. In the midst of these hallucinations or other irritating external stimuli, stay grounded and curious. Note all these potentially difficult sensations and visions as outer Shadow qualities and then notice how you feel and react to them as inner Shadow qualities.

Guiding Others at This Stage of the Journey with Impeccability

If you are guiding a client on a journey at this stage, you can take on the important role of being an anchor through reassurance. Let your voyager know that they will be okay, that they will make it back into Ordinary Reality after this journey. Be available for hand holding or certain comforting touch, but also be sure to agree ahead of time what type of touch would be appropriate for reassurance.

Gently remind them to recall their Intent statement and make meaning of the experience through that lens. Think of yourself as a *doula* (midwife) of the voyager's psychedelic birth. You are there to help provide a deep well of peace amidst the stormy waters of the psyche's deconstruction.

An experienced guide can be in altered states with the voyager without ingesting any plant medicine, as per the old phrase "contact high." However, as stated before, the Huichol teaching is that the guide would always take some of the medicine, even if a smaller dose, to meet and honor this particular entheogenic consciousness.

When you become adept as a guide in your own psyche, you not only relate to your own inner world of memories and reflections but also accurately track the consciousness of others. Thus, the skill of the advanced guide is tracking the consciousness of each member in a group journey accurately over the entire time of the journey.

Keep in mind that it takes years of training to be able to distinguish one's own Shadow material from that of the other, while at the same time experiencing the complete interbeing with the voyager's psyche.

That is why we continually stress the importance of doing one's Shadow work diligently through the deep and thorough training of the Journey to Completion.

In order to become an impeccable guide, you must be able to hold and integrate your own Shadow material over and over again. This prevents you from becoming triggered and pulled into other people's unhealed issues in the psychedelic space where the lines between self and other are more blurred. It also prevents projections and misuse of power.

An adept guide will be receptive to interacting with the voyager in a respectful way, not a dominating or overly directive way. The guide should work to keep the voyager focused on their Intent to encounter certain shadows and help them continue to trust what is being revealed and what the plant is allowing them to know.

Being a guide is a huge responsibility because, essentially, you are holding someone else's psyche in a fragile state. When someone is opened up by plant medicines, they are more susceptible to suggestion and manipulation. Even if you are entering the role of guide with good Intentions and a kind heart, if you haven't healed certain wounded parts of yourself, you are susceptible to misuse of power and unintentionally implant warped perspectives and ideas into those you are guiding.

Within these cautionary comments, you can also hear the utmost importance of choosing your guide wisely and carefully. Pay attention to any red flags beforehand, as these can be helpful Threshold Guardians warning you not to proceed. Don't be afraid or too polite to back out of working with them at any point.

NORMA'S Example of Guiding a Group Intent

In one group I led, the participants at this stage kept engaging in casual small talk and sharing mundane stories from their daily lives. It was pleasant conversation and yet, when it had gone on for over an hour, I recognized that the constant chatter was a way of avoiding the uncomfortable feelings they were having beneath the surface. I gently said, "This is one way to do this journey. It is comfortable. But you might be resisting some deeper knowing." I reminded the group to focus on their Intents. They had not come just to make conversation; they had entered this particular journey to come into contact with a deep power that resided within each one of them. When they each individually remembered their particular Intents, they were able to transition into a deeper level and gain great insight from the journey.

Taking Self-Responsibility as a Guide

As a guide, it can be challenging to know how much or how little to direct the journey and where your voyager travels. There is no steadfast rule to how much you guide versus how much you take a back seat.

Many programs that teach facilitation opt for the "hands-off" approach. In this school of thought, the guide is more of a "space holder," someone who ensures that everyone is safe but discourages much dialogue or processing of what is arising. They are there to hold the space but are encouraged not to let the participants talk or move too much. In this role, the purpose of the guide is to continually direct the journey into an inward process.

It makes sense that without proper psychonavigation training, this would be a safe route to how to guide without damage. If one doesn't know the intricacies of Shadow work within the psychedelic experience and how the psyche works, this is the best answer.

After becoming adept at working with the psyche in a healed and lucid way, you can be more directive in plant medicine journeys. When you know you are not triggered or overriding people from a Shadow place in yourself, then you can help them work through their own stuck places with integrity. This careful intervention is about the right or impeccable use of power.

When you holistically engage with your psyche in altered states of being you learn the terrain of the psyche. Although everyone's minds and inner worlds are different, there is a collective unconscious, as Carl

Jung refers to it, that all people share. Learning the paths, valleys, and roads of the unconscious helps you to better navigate others' minds.

Taking self-responsibility is essential when acting as a guide. It's important to constantly be questioning how you are leading. A true leader will be a part of the community, not holding themselves over others but being accountable to feedback. Furthermore, training in Non-violent Communication skills can be very helpful when learning to be a guide. It helps you to speak in such a way as to bring about connection rather than having to be right, and thus, avoiding getting stuck in the realms of blame/shame.

Non-dualism is central to this type of work. If you are stuck in a place of viewing the world as black and white, right and wrong, you will judge your voyagers and lay your trip on their journeys. When you can graduate from the dualistic way of viewing the world we are inculcated into, you are better able to meet people in their traumas with compassion and skill.

From a non-dualistic framework, you can carefully investigate what is arising in all its complexities and help them do the alchemical work of transmuting the Shadow material into gold.

Ground Yourself in Your Essential Goodness

The Huichol teach their children to value what they call their Essence Self (primary state of consciousness). Rather than coming in with "original sin," as we are taught through the Catholic lineage, children are told that they have no sins. We all come in with an essential goodness at the core of who we are.

The Huichol do teach about how we accumulate sins that need to be cleansed before and through ceremonies; however, the word "sin" can be very weighted. In this context, think of sin as those traumatized and fragmented parts of ourselves that are split off from our Persona. They represent parts of ourselves that we need to forgive and heal. When we move toward non-dualism, even so-called "sins" are not evil—they are the broken parts in ourselves that need mending, the places where we have misused our power and had power misused against us.

If you have grown up in a culture emphasizing original sin instead of original blessing, you have to do remedial work in order to remember your essential goodness and cultivate self-love. You also have to work at not immediately reverting to a blaming stance toward others.

As John Bradshaw, a well-known psychologist in the addiction recovery field was known to say, our Western white culture is steeped in blaming and shaming as its main defense mechanism. **This effort to grow away from dualism and toward a genuine ability to hold the paradoxes and complexities long enough without coming to premature foreclosure is a skill that shamanic cultures have taught for centuries.**

NORMA'S Example of Facing Past Traumas and Coming into Non-dualistic Awareness

My work with the Huichol and plant medicine carried me into the stage of deconstruction and hard memories.

For many years I was a leader in the domestic violence intervention movement and had witnessed horrendous abuse of women and children. In this plant medicine journey, all of those memories came rushing in. I began to cry uncontrollably, wondering how humans could act in such evil ways. Why did so much suffering exist on planet Earth?

I cried until no tears were left in my body and tossed the last tissue into the fire. I felt my despair sink into a bottomless free-fall, into an abyss of darkness. I began to frantically dig in the dirt. I saw all the faces of the abused women come vividly before my eyes.

I just wanted to die under the weight of that suffering. With the wise guidance of my Huichol and Navajo teachers, I was carefully held within that experience all the way through to the other side of my despair. However, it was not an easy process. I had to go fully into the Shadow and hold it unwaveringly for many hours until I came through to a perception where the paradox of human evil and love merged into a beatific vision.

After that, I could see through the eyes of "wholeness and reconciliation" that my rational mind could not have attained on its own.

Indeed, one of the main purposes of psilocybin, ayahuasca, peyote, and other fungi/plant allies is to bring up the Shadow, the wounded places for healing. Journeys that seek to avoid the Shadow may be leaving out the most essential gift the entheogens bring us.

Mystical traditions have ways of addressing this shadowy stage of perception. For example, Medieval mystic Meister Eckhart dramatically spoke to this when he said, "Eventually you have to trust God to kill you." "Kill" in this sense means deconstructing your ego defense mechanisms, the identity that has provided a sense of safety. It comes to the point where our defended bulwarks keep us separated and alone. The Shadow protective mechanisms, working well for a time, eventually become dysfunctional and very costly. We must trust that the deconstruction, painful as it is at the time, leads through to a greater wholeness that is life-generating.

37

Working with the Shadow in the Psychedelic Journey

As we know, psilocybin and other entheogens most often bring out shadow material so the choice to engage with them necessitates adequate shadow work skills.

When you start out on a plant medicine journey, if you are trained in the Journey to Completion method, you recognize that your Outer Shadow might be triggered and your Inner Shadow's defensive reactions appear, (see page 53 for Outer/Inner Shadow Chart). This could be literal—for example, you start to see the guide as your oppressive father or smothering mother. It can also appear in the form of visions and memories that are surfacing. For example, you could unearth a memory of an incident wherein your parent dominated you and then be catapulted back into a childlike part of you while wrestling with the effects of the plant medicine. Psilocybin can shape-shift your vision to see fearful things in the faces of those around you. You can have difficult images arise within your own mind.

Understanding that Outer Shadow figures or challenging visions are likely to appear during the journey allows you to approach them with curiosity rather than being overwhelmed by fear, just as you do when dealing with a nightmare in a lucid dream state. Instead of being caught off guard by these difficult encounters, you can enter the experience ready to address them.

You embrace these encounters because you recognize that this is an ideal opportunity to work on transforming and healing the stuck areas within yourself, with the psychedelic medicine serving as your ally in this process. Shifting away from a dualistic mindset, you perceive the people and situations that arise not as adversaries to blame but as symbolic guides highlighting what needs healing. You can even express gratitude toward those representing old wounds for bringing attention to areas requiring your healing.

With the Outer/Inner Shadow understanding, the voyager is free to go ahead and name whatever they experience. When the guide is trained in the Journey to Completion methodology, they will not take this naming personally, even if it has to do with them and how they are acting. The guide will work with this *transference* to help you understand your experience more fully. You can welcome whatever shadows arise because you trust that these images are here to deliver the message you need.

Even if you aren't trained in the Journey to Completion, simply understanding that the Shadow will emerge—and knowing how to engage with it constructively, rather than taking it personally or fearing it—prepares you to be a more effective guide or explorer of the psyche.

Recognizing the need for boundaries and containment when someone expresses their Shadow in a group setting is essential. It's not about allowing unchecked projections without resolution. When a guide points out others' Shadows without proper support, they exert undue control over the group. As you've learned, it's crucial to avoid leaders who misuse their power to dominate or elevate themselves above others. A skilled leader navigates the Shadow, empowering everyone to recognize and address their own Shadow at their own pace, with the goal of achieving resolution and a more comprehensive, healed perspective.

Here is a case example of a difficult situation and what to do when someone goes out of the boundaries you have set:

NORMA'S Example of Group Work

In this Shadow-evoking stage of the journey, I was leading a group of six people. We were all sitting, and everyone was in their internal processes.

Suddenly, one man got up and went over to the area where we had stored the food for after the journey. He took a beautiful pie that a woman had made, put his hand in it, and gouged out a big scoop of it to eat. It was a relatively small but still aggressive act, and it was directed toward the woman who made the pie. He had seemed triggered by her in earlier discussions, and this was the moment where the Shadow took hold and led him to direct aggression toward her.

I addressed the boundary crossing and asked him to come and join us back in the living room, yet he was still very agitated. He revealed that the woman who made the pie was reminding him of his mother. The woman was very sad and angry that he had damaged her pie.

He continued to be agitated. Luckily, I had a co-leader and was able to divide the group into two sections and take them into separate rooms to each deal with their pain and Shadow triggers and projections.

After about two hours of grounding and processing in the smaller groups, we returned to join the whole group. We worked with the man who had done the aggressive action and the woman who had been hurt by it, each individually to look at the Shadow projections and name them as that.

Freeing them both from the trap of blame, we were able to put the microcosm of this interaction into the bigger picture of the people in their past that they were being reminded of in the current situation. With more acknowledgment of what was going on, we were able to bring a loving presence to both of them. We focused the group's consciousness on loving and accepting him.

He lay down on the floor in the middle of the room, and we asked permission to touch his feet, head, and hands. Held in love, he began to realize that he had been sexually abused as a boy and his mother had not known or intervened to help him. His body convulsed with sobs of pain, and he recounted the incident to us in vivid recollection.

We had a powerful therapeutic healing focus time on him for several hours to follow. The woman whose pie was damaged was also a sexual abuse survivor and got attention for her feelings, too.

Both of these individuals had been in therapy with me for a year leading up to this moment and continued to be for several years after this session, so I was able to bring them through to deeper healing even after the journey. Approaching the plant medicine journey in this way, incorporating the Shadow healing work, enabled a true integration of what arose in the psychedelic journey to occur.

Many people seek the best methods for integrating their plant medicine journeys. Our response to is that a comprehensive, integrative framework with a whole-systems approach to the entire journey is needed; otherwise, it is difficult for the mind to make connections and maintain the thread of the Shadow pattern being healed.

The Journey to Completion offers a model for such an approach, encompassing everything "from the doorway in, to the doorway out." You are currently acquiring essential elements of this framework: learning how to prepare for the journey by studying and navigating your psyche beforehand, understanding how to address Shadow aspects that emerge during the journey, and discovering the appropriate tools to integrate the experience afterward.

38

Client Case Studies

CASE STUDY 1 –
Journey to the Realms of Death:
A Rite of Passage

Sita is a young professional woman, aged 23, seeking a rite of passage into adulthood. In the screening session, she presents as very astute psychologically and mature for her age. She reports no previous psychological or physical health concerns.

She took psilocybin once in a recreational way with friends in college. It was not such a good experience, as there was no *set and setting* consideration; that is, safe psychological, social, and cultural parameters in place prior to entering the psychedelic experience.

They were at a party, and at a certain point in the evening, she felt she had to leave the party atmosphere and go outside to be alone—the group seemed like zombies to her, and she was not feeling safe with any of them. So she left her friends and went off by herself and felt that she was sinking into a grave and dying for many hours. She experienced a devastating feeling of abandonment. There was no one to rescue her or be with her through that hard night. She said that she had felt abandoned by the Universe.

Sita wanted to address that first psychedelic experience by doing psilocybin in an Intentional way, one that would allow her to receive healing from the previous difficult experience. Her Intent during the ceremony was to be held in a sacred container that would allow her to feel safer and more productive and bring a sense of spiritual connection and direction to her life.

The ceremony with a group of eight was held over an entire weekend. Many of the participants had journeyed together before and knew one another quite deeply. It was a group of all women of varying ages. Everyone was approaching the plant medicine with a spiritual Intent setting and had been through a preliminary individual screening session with the co-facilitators.

Set and Setting

The ceremony was held at a beautiful remote cabin in a wooded setting. The group met on Friday evening for a shared meal and an informal discussion of their Intentions for the weekend. The plant medicine journey was to begin on Saturday afternoon and continue into the night. Sunday was intended to be a time of gradual integration followed by ritual clean-up and closing of the sacred space. On Saturday morning each participant had time to walk in nature to connect with the surrounding environment and to journal and do divination readings to clarify their Intent and become quiet and mindful.

When we sat in a circle on Saturday afternoon, a beautiful altar was created, with each person contributing meaningful objects they had brought with them or found. We then did a drumming-induced trance journey to bring everyone into connection with their inner guidance system and feel a sense of the presence of their power animal. Each person then spoke their Intent aloud to the group so that everyone was aware of one another's issues and intended purpose in doing this ceremony. Then the psilocybin plant medicine was passed around, and each person took some.

At first, people were casually sitting back as the medicine took effect. The facilitator led a drumming-induced symbolic canoe ceremony. During a canoe ceremony, everyone sits in formation as though sitting in a canoe, with each person located in a different symbolic place in the canoe.

Sita sat in the middle, with rowers on each side. That was the position of the princess or precious cargo of the canoe. At one point, as the medicine took effect, she started slumping backward and was caught by the woman behind her. We were all concerned. She looked very pale and gaunt. The drummer kept drumming, and the women held her gently and put a pillow under her head. It seemed as if she was losing consciousness.

When asked how she was, she said that she was seeing nothingness; whether her eyes were open or closed, she saw only blackness, not people, not objects in the room. She was entirely surrounded visually by blackness and a sense of being in a zone of great emptiness. She feared that she was physically dying and was afraid that she had taken an overdose. But she had not taken an unusually large dose—the same amount as others.

Then she felt negative spirits coming toward her. They felt very threatening and menacing. She feared that they were going to take her away into the death zone. She was quiet but writhing in agony and seemed to have neurological twitches.

How Norma Dealt with This Situation

Several women held Sita and closely attended to her throughout the hours that followed as she returned from the dark zones. It took her about two hours to be present to that bleak liminality. During that time, we ascertained that she was going to be okay, because her color returned, she was conscious and talking, and she was able to move her body. One woman had beautiful ways of encouraging her to surrender to the experience, and that seemed to help her trust into it just as it was.

We had one person who had not taken any plant medicine who could keep ministering to everyone's needs and reassuring Sita that everything was going to be fine. She brought water and attended to all of our needs.

As Sita began emerging from the strongest effects of the medicine, she shared with us many frightening memories of a date-rape situation and other times when she had been very alone and afraid. Then her visions altered, and she was seeing many more positive hallucinogenic visions of union and allyship. For example, she saw each person as visually altered and appearing as their power animals, and the words spoken by each one seemed to magically meet her exact thoughts and needs.

She felt as if she was being ushered down a long, swirling tunnel and then had the visceral experience of being reborn into an all-white room.

In this room, she was gently received and held by the women in the group, who seemed as though they were all floating in another dimension with her. She felt as if it was some otherworldly, heavenly realm. In this cosmic dimension, Sita sensed not only the humans in the group but many kind beings coming to help her, attending to her every need. She described a feeling of being like a queen in a place of all-knowing and great compassion. She felt the great care of the Universe for her.

Then she had the vivid sense of the presence of Our Lady of Guadalupe. She felt a loving closeness to this divine mother, the beloved patron saint of Mexico, and put a shawl over her own head and took on the appearance of Guadalupe.

At this point, the group was moving outside in the early morning hours to sit by a bonfire and sip tea and quietly chat. Sita spoke of the meaning of her journey, and how she felt so met by the comfort of this group of women and was able to experience a profound healing of her past wound of abandonment and loneliness. She felt an integration of herself with her power, because she had been met by the divine mother companion Guadalupe. Her power animal in the drumming journey was the hawk, and a hawk auspiciously circled overhead as we talked around the fire.

The ritual space had been held safely, and Sita's desire to have this experience be a rite of passage for her was beautifully accomplished. A rite of passage implies going into the Underworld, experiencing a deconstruction of identity, receiving a gift, then ascending into a positive reconstruction of the identity. This journey was very powerful for Sita, and several years later, in a check-in session, she reported that it had been a key, guiding moment for her sense of life purpose and remains an anchor for her soul.

CASE STUDY 2 – Small Group Interactive Session

Beth is a social worker living in a small town in the Pacific Northwest. She wanted to experience a psychedelic journey because of the current publicity about the use of psilocybin in the therapeutic treatment of depression and wanted to be able to lead her clients in these psychedelic sessions. She had not had psychedelic experiences previously but does admit to periodic excessive use of alcohol.

She was cheerful and chatty in the group and presented a positive image of her current nuclear family life—she is married to a successful business owner and they have two children. Beth shared that in regard to her family of origin, she was raised in a strict family. Her mother was cold and critical and her dad was distant. Both of them were college professors. They had high expectations of her, and she did well in school. She said that she is a strong, go-getter but has not received the emotional nurturance she needs.

Set and Setting

We were meeting in a house with a group of colleagues, and everyone knew each other well. It was a safe and trusting environment and community of friends. The space was private, and no outside disturbances were present.

As the plant medicine took effect, she became very talkative in the group and making lots of jokes. She seemed to need to keep talking and moving about. Even while others were silent, she kept talking and did get some to join in with her in merrymaking and laughing. She talked a lot about the effects of the psilocybin and wanted others to share what was happening in their visions. She became very flirtatious with a man in the group whose wife was also present and they laughed and joked in a teasing way.

She physically draped her body over two of the men in the group as she laughed and joked. Finally, I suggested that she take some quiet time and focus inward. She became quiet for a short time but seemed agitated and then wanted to talk again.

She gradually revealed things about her relationship with her husband that were not so good yet spoke in cryptic ways. Eventually, as I listened and asked questions, she began to reveal that she was being physically beaten by her husband and that she had tried to get away but could not. She said that she had never talked about this to anyone before. They are both respected in their community, so she was afraid to speak out and felt guilty for bringing it up here.

She got into a very sad, emotional state, crying and feeling afraid to return to her home. We were thankful that she was finally speaking to her real needs and what was causing her anxiety and agitation. As the medicine wore off, we spoke of things she can possibly do to get safety and help when she returns. After the session, she attended two follow-up sessions for integration but then wanted to move on to be able to facilitate psilocybin with her clients and did not want to focus on her personal issues anymore. The facilitator recommended that she continue to address her relationship trauma issues more adequately before leading others in plant medicine journeys.

How Norma Dealt with This Situation

To manage her joking and acting-out behaviors, I gently asked Beth why she was joking so much and asked whether she was avoiding something she wanted to explore. I asked everyone to sit together, so that each person would receive the focus and attention of the group while they spoke about whatever they wanted to work on in themselves. In that way, the facilitator can redirect the energy and take control of the focus of the group mind. When it came time for Beth to have her turn as the focus of attention, at first she tried to joke around, but the others were focused and ready to listen to her more deeply. This helped her begin to admit what was really going on that she was trying to avoid. She eventually admitted the seriousness of the problems in her marital relationship and was met with great compassion from the group members. The playfulness had been a good way to meet her initially, and this desire to be present for her turned into a deep caring and concern on her behalf. There was a sense of union among the group, as each one shared their own Shadow or difficult issues and felt met by the wise listening presence of the facilitator and the group members. Beth felt less shame and was able to be present with the true dilemma of her situation and felt empowered to seek more help when she returned to her home environment.

39

Emerging – The Gentle Glide Back

As mythologist Joseph Campbell once noted, it was necessary for him to journey into liminal space for a long time, living out in the mountains for five years, before he could return genuinely knowing that the Universe is a friendly place. Emerging from the liminal space of the psychedelic Dreamtime from a plant medicine journey can often be a pleasant and illuminating time. If you encountered the shadows and fears that arose, faced them, and gained some profound insights, a great peace can flood in at this moment.

At this stage, if this is a group ceremony, it can be a bonding experience to pass a talking stick and ask everyone to focus their attention on one person at a time. Everyone is still in a slightly altered state and, therefore, able to feel with the subtle awareness of their primary consciousness. The person who has the focus takes their turn to speak aloud reflections on their journey experience. What often results is a remarkable sense of oneness among the group. Generally speaking, an abundance of warmhearted closeness naturally occurs at the end of the ceremony.

If you are on a journey by yourself, it can also be a great moment to write down your reflections. Catching them before you return fully to ordinary consciousness can be profound, because much like after a dream, sometimes the realizations will fade from memory as you return to Ordinary Reality.

This is the time for gentle rest, ease, and quiet chatting with others as you sip on some tea. It is important to re-ground into your body. The sensations will return to normal, yet they may feel quite tender or even raw. Food can be brought out—just a piece of fruit and some nuts, or homemade soup, for example; something nurturing. And do drink water.

When you have the water in hand, you can also use it to do the wonderful ritual act that Guadalupe did for us when I studied with her. She went around with a cool cloth and wiped our brow and the back of our neck in a tender, loving way.

It is a good time to review the Intent you named before beginning your journey. Ask yourself if your Intent was accomplished and reflect on what shadows presented themselves. Through going on this journey, a range of wise insights may have been gained about your life purpose. A newfound sense of clarity and purity is common at this stage.

Your usual identity will slowly return but generally, you are not as attached to that identity as you were before. You have been loosened up from your typical habits of perception. If you've accomplished healing while in the psychedelic Underworld, you should feel free from the distortions of your previous Shadow/trauma-laden perspectives. Some people in your group may want to discuss the insights they gained and how the dots got connected in their minds; others may not, but either one is fine.

When physical conditions are related to psychosomatic responses, complete or partial cures of physical ailments can also happen. One woman we guided had chronic lower back pain for years. After the session, in which we worked through her memories of having been abused as a young child, the back pain was gone and did not return. This is a time when the guide can gently encourage the voyager to listen closely to their body. When we allow the body to unburden itself, who knows what miracles might come?

It is also a good time to build a link between this moment and the Ordinary Reality state of mind you left behind when first entering this extraordinary realm. For example, look again at the art you made beforehand or the tarot cards you drew at the Intent-setting stage. Oftentimes, you will glean a deeper understanding from the symbols on the cards and the images you created from the symbolic realms of your psyche.

Clean-Up: Proper Closing of the Portal

We have opened a sacred container, a portal that took us out of Ordinary Reality into the liminal space of non-Ordinary Reality. When you are coming back into Ordinary Reality after a psychedelic journey, closing the portal is just as important as opening it. To close the portal requires that you fully re-ground in the present; as with drumming journeys, you want to make sure you bring all parts of yourself all the way back through to the other side. Oftentimes, when people feel fragmented or "spun out" after a journey, it is because they've forgotten the important step of bringing themselves all the way back and closing the portal mindfully.

At the end of a journey into multi-dimensional consciousness, we must return to kneel and touch the earth. Michael Meade, a mythologist and storyteller, often says that Westerners tend to discount this very important final beat of the initiatory journey. The final beat, which is just as important as the others, is the Return. In fact, to quote Frank Herbert's science fiction novel *Dune*, now a movie: "The Journey *is* in the Return."

The closing ritual is a time to make sure to get fully re-grounded in the present. That's why it's good to begin to express words of gratitude and share what you have gathered. As with drumming journeys, narrating, step by step, the story of your plant medicine experience to the group or your guide is a way to ground your consciousness back into Ordinary Reality. When we make an effort to speak of the beauty, and the gifts received, it's a way of honoring the medicine.

When sharing your journey, it's crucial to establish and uphold healthy, clear dynamics during this time. As with sharing your dreams, it is not about having another person interpret your journey for you; meaning-making is your task. This ensures that a potentially therapeutic experience doesn't turn into a source of additional conflict. After a psychedelic journey, individuals are often emotionally sensitive and vulnerable, so feedback from therapists or facilitators can have a significant and lasting impact; therefore, it's important to provide a space for open sharing without interruptions, interpretations, or analysis, allowing participants to express their experiences freely and safely.

A Suggestion for the Closing Ritual of a Ceremonial Journey

- **Stand in a Circle** – Each person speaks briefly about what they experienced and offers words of gratitude for the ceremony and the container that was created.
- **Sing Songs and Prayers of Gratitude** – These can be sung together to create a harmonic resonance of heart-focused gratitude in the collective field.
- **The Guide Gives Admonitions and Instructions for Reentry:**
  - **Do not rush things** – For example, the Huichol require that you not return to your daily obligations and duties for five days.
  - **Practice the change in perspective as you go out into your life** You are instructed on how to continue viewing your reality through the new lens you were gifted as a result of ingesting the altering substances.
- **Have a Feast of Some Sort Once the Portal is Closed** – Eating together one final time bookends the adventure you just went on alone or with a group.
- **Everyone Disassembles The Altar Together and Cleans The Ritual Space.**

The closing of the portal and finishing of the psychedelic effects is not the end of the voyage; it's just the beginning. The real work and honoring of the journey is to live out, step by step, your changed perspective in your ordinary life. To walk the path with heart in service to the highest good of all is a valid proof of having fully digested the plant medicine's gift. There's the immediate closing, the closing that can happen over the next few days and weeks, and the closing that happens over the years. Each medicine journey gives us a lot to integrate. That is why it is important to slow down in our culture obsessed with the next "fix" and take the appropriate amount of time for integration. Groups often plan to get together a week or two later to check in with each other and further process their insights.

Conclusion

Knowing others is intelligence; knowing yourself is true wisdom.
Mastering others is strength; mastering yourself is true power.

—LAO TZU, Tao Te Ching

We have shown you this initiatory pathway; now it is up to you to practice the art of navigating your inner world. Experiential knowledge is essential. You must discover the unique map within your own psyche. The teachings in this book have equipped you with tangible tools and techniques to integrate these practices into your daily life. We've shared maps of consciousness—templates that embrace the wild within.

This well-trodden pathway is a template, a codex, that once discovered must become embedded in your heart. You do this by continually walking this path of self-responsible introspection, then it becomes an archetypal "path of heart" clearly established within your own psyche.

This ancient pathway serves to link human consciousness over time and space. As with mycelial networks, the vast interconnectivity of humans in the Dreamtime is real. Humanity is designed to explore these expansive inner dimensions. Each of us cycles through both ordinary consciousness and the Dreamtime on a daily basis, which means that psychonavigation is not only our birthright but an absolute necessity.

Now that so many people are being invited to explore their consciousness through psychedelics with little fear of punishment, there is a growing need for skilled navigators who can learn to become skilled guides for others. Following the Journey to Completion Map discussed in this book insures your safety in your otherworldly encounters; it gives you the tools to stalk and sequester your Shadow so that "slippery fish" does not delude or overpower you. The codex of this "meta map" allows you to see the entire container, and this is what allows safe passage in and out of the vast otherworlds of non-ordinary time and space. As emphasized, it's essential not just to learn these practices but to actively engage in them, both in your nightly dream work and daily life. Committing to this spiritual path and following it in a disciplined way will allow you to reap the benefits of your studies.

Now that you've completed this book, consider making the teachings offered here into a regular practice:

- **Drumming Journey Trance Induction**: Do this at least once a week to strengthen your ability to connect with your inner guidance system.
- **Dreaming and Lucid Dreaming Practices**: Diligently do the daytime and nighttime dream practices to gather personal power and agency in your dreams and waking life.
- **Intent Setting**: Every day in your waking reality set your intention to be fully awake. Especially when in altered-state explorations, use the power of a clear Intent. This practice will reinforce your ability to be in synchronistic flow with the Universe.
- **Shadow Study**: Make a habit of humble self-reflection rather than blaming others.
- **Entheogens**: When working with plant medicines, use the methods we have shared for understanding potential shadows to navigate challenging experiences more effectively.

Through polyphasic awareness, you gain a big-picture perspective on the interconnectedness of ordinary and non-ordinary realities. This, in turn, allows you to see that psychonavigation is not just limited to altered states; it plays a vital role in all phases of awareness. This is the art of lucid living.

Ultimately, you've been given a road map to personal empowerment and spiritual growth, allowing you to harness the transformative potential of your psyche and imagination. As you continue to navigate your inner world, the process of individuation—integrating various parts of the psyche in order to achieve wholeness—will unfold.

By embracing all aspects of your psyche, even those you once found undesirable, you are setting an example. You can become a beacon of light. You can become a human who thinks and acts with the right use of power for the highest good of all at any particular moment. What could be a more worthwhile calling than to be someone who aspires to move in the inner and outer worlds of energy with a high standard of impeccability?

We will now provide a summary of what you've learned in this book, so you can continue to integrate this knowledge into your life.

The Art of Psychonavigation

Through the art of accurately understanding your position within the psyche and planning a route through your inner terrains, you become a true psychonaut. When you practice directly encountering and learning from your psyche, you enter into an honest dialogue with the depths of yourself and what is yours to heal.

Navigating the liminal realms of the psyche involves harnessing the power of imagination positively. While imagination can often lead to worry and negative scenarios, it can also be reclaimed as a tool for empowerment. Working with your imagination during the day while in Ordinary Reality prepares you to not let your imagination run away in altered states.

When you redirect this creative energy, you transform the mind from an enemy into an ally, using your imagination to heal distorted perceptions. You will then be gifted with a change in perspective. Seeing through new eyes will then allow you to act in ways that radically shift the world around you.

Psychonavigation allows for the wise integration of the conscious and subconscious, leading to a more balanced and fulfilled sense of self. Learning how to navigate your psyche through drumming journeys and lucid dreaming can bring a new level of richness and cohesion to your plant medicine experiences. When you practice navigating your psyche regularly, you can engage in ever deeper "meaning-making" and thus, bring back profound psychological gifts from the Underworld of the plant medicine journey.

Honoring the Lineage

The journey of spiritual growth is deeply rooted in the contributions of our elders and teachers. Acknowledging these contributions is more than giving credit; it taps into the potent energy of our lineage and the part we play in its healing.

By recognizing the power and strength of those who came before us, we embrace our responsibility toward those who follow. Explore the imprints of your familial lineage with regard to how you navigate the Dreamtime and the deeper layers of your psyche. To be a skilled psychonavigator requires you to undertake the necessary personal Shadow work to mend past wounds that reside in your lineage.

Think of all the wise teachings that have led you to where you currently stand. Take time to honor those who have contributed vast domains of information to your practice. They are a part of you. You do not arise out of nothing, and you do not own everything you take in. *Paticcasamupada*, the interdependent co-arising of all phenomena, according to Sanskrit texts, is the truth of our existence. We live within a vast system of reciprocal exchange on planet Earth.

Scrutinize how you talk about information you pass along. Are you making sure that you name and give credit to the lineages? It is especially important to give credit to voices that are typically subjugated, such as women and people of color, because historically, their knowledge has been stolen and appropriated. Contrary to what is practiced in an extractive, colonizing culture, owning your lineage fully and accurately actually gives you more credibility, not less.

CONCLUSION

Inner Guidance – You Are Not Alone Inside Your Mind

From a spiritual perspective, psychonavigation facilitates the "I–Thou" relationship. In altered states of consciousness, we encounter a presence beyond the mundane self, leading to the profound *gnosis*, or lived experience of being connected with Higher Consciousness.

When we connect to the divine other, the "Thou" within our innermost self, we are no longer venturing into challenging terrain alone. We can find new levels of empowerment by knowing that we have first-hand experience of something greater than the small "I," the ego.

With the support of this "I–Thou" relationship, we gain inner guidance on where to go within our psyche. Ancient teachings give us a deep understanding of how this inner "Thou" comes to us in the form of a power animal, a very real "other" consciousness that guides us toward our wise use of power. In states of lucidity, our power animal points us to the appropriate past wounds that are ripe for healing and protects us from going too far, too fast. Connecting to that wise animal consciousness helps us not only carefully navigate our psyche but also become more aware and strategic in everyday situations. With a strong intuition intact and a connection with the inner "Thou" relationship, we become more confident in our decisions and inner knowing of what is right for us. Synchronicities and coincidences that show up in ordinary reality will confirm that we are on the right track and accurately listening to our inner guidance.

Entering Liminal Awareness through Drumming Journeys

As you've learned, shamanic drumming is a key practice in mysticism in cultures around the world, facilitating a trance state that allows for deep inner exploration. This practice has been validated by both Indigenous cultures and modern science, which recognizes the impact of rhythmic sound on the brain. Drumming can synchronize the hemispheres of the brain, creating a unified state of consciousness that enhances spiritual and mental clarity.

You have learned a map for successfully entering and safely returning from the Underworld with a drumming journey. By following this specific pattern, you can carefully descend into the earthy, embodied, subterranean zones of the Underworld and come back up. Once you understand the specific route to take, you can navigate more confidently in these realms.

Now that you have a clear outline of how to safely walk in and out of the Underworld through the drumbeat, regularly take on the practice of going on drumming journeys. As with dreams, each journey will be unique and uncover hidden things within your psyche you may not have been aware of before. Drumming journeys train the mind to maintain lucid awareness while venturing into altered, non-ordinary states.

Waking up in the Dream: Lucid Dreaming

When you go to sleep each night, you have the potential to "wake up." In the case of psychonavigation, the ability to become lucid within your dream presents a profound opportunity to work directly with your psyche and come face to face with the suppressed or unconscious parts of yourself.

Working on energetic difficulties and mental limitations within your dream produces a flexibility of mind that is a primary goal within many wisdom traditions, including Tibetan Dream Yoga. A flexible mind overcomes the limitations of what Buddhism terms "wrong views," which constrict experience and keep us trapped in habitual cycles of behavior. True freedom, or empowered agency, comes from liberating the psyche from its stuck places. This practice of lucidity is a lifelong journey, one where we are continually assessing and freeing up the rigid places of the mind. Connecting with your Dreamtime isn't about running away from the reality of mundane life; quite the opposite. Honoring the Dreamtime is about realizing the interconnectedness between the world of dreams and that of waking reality—one does not exist without the other. Achieving a good balance between these realms is the accomplishment of an adept psychonavigator.

Entering the Psychedelic Dreamtime

Once you've ingested the plant medicine, you are entering a state of consciousness akin to dreaming, where the Dreamtime begins to merge with waking reality. This transition can be gradual or swift, blurring the lines between Ordinary Reality and the Dreamtime. You find yourself in a liminal space—what Celtic shamans called "betwixt and between"—letting go of one state of consciousness and moving toward another. In that state, it is crucial to recall your training on how to stay conscious in these liminal spaces.

Remember that you should not enter the Unknown without a clear intent. It will help you maintain lucidity as the world around you starts to deconstruct and shape-shift. As you delve deeper into the psychedelic Dreamtime, it is vital to approach intense experiences with surrender and curiosity, embracing the *gnosis* that arises from "direct knowing."

One reason to undertake a psychedelic journey is the opportunity to confront and heal Shadow material, bringing wholeness and reconciliation through the deconstruction of ego defense mechanisms. By trusting the process and embracing the complexities of human consciousness, you open yourself to profound healing and insights, ultimately connecting with your essential goodness. Our Huichol teachers always reminded us before a plant medicine journey that we were doing this to become adept at walking the path with heart, for the highest good of all.

Integrating Your Shadow

"Individuation," a Jungian psychology concept, is the process of integrating various parts of the psyche to achieve wholeness. For example, each of us must do deep work in order to heal and balance our inner masculine and inner feminine parts.

The Shadow integration process is an integral part of individuation. It involves uncovering and integrating the hidden aspects of the self that were buried long ago as a way of protecting ourselves. Accurate and skillful navigation tools are a must in order to safely transmute these Shadow elements.

By following the Journey to Completion Map, you learn that there is a systematic and holistic approach to transmuting the Shadow material. In this book, you learned how to begin working with the Shadow in various realms of consciousness. Undertaken in a step-by-step, organic way, the practices of lucid dreaming, trance-induced drumming journeys, and more intentional use of psychedelics will lead you to a life with more integrity.

As you achieve more and more wholeness within yourself, healing and welcoming back the "cast out" parts of yourself, you become a more accurate and effective navigator of the psyche. Eventually, with enough inner work and Shadow integration, you will be ready to guide others into their psyches in an impeccable way.

However, in order to facilitate the altered-state journeys of other people, you must first be clear within yourself that you will not misuse your power. The hallmark of the ancient Indigenous teachings we present here is that we do our own Shadow integration work adequately before presuming to lead others on their journeys.

The Journey Continues

You have now been exposed to the foundational tools to engage with your psyche consciously and carefully. As you continue to discover the hidden places within your mind/body, you will find that the journey is one that never ends. It is expansive and eternal. And yet, with each step you take, you are making progress toward a unified mind, a more coherent consciousness that is no longer scattered, fragmented, or suppressed.

As the psyche heals and strengthens, presence and equanimity become the baseline, regardless of the challenges we face in the external world. Life will always present us with new lessons and obstacles to overcome. Completion is not about reaching a state where nothing difficult ever happens to us again; rather, it's about being able to face these hardships directly and regard them as gifts offering us the next level of personal empowerment and growth.

CONCLUSION

When you have these effective, ancient tools to work with, it's no longer just about "thinking" your way out of life's struggles; instead, it is about systematically taking on each Shadow pattern and lesson and working through the mind/body to a non-dualistic, authentic integration. The Huichol call this joining of our higher self being a "one-hearted human."

Furthermore, we highly recommend that if you want lasting growth and permanent change in your life, you find a master teacher to guide you. Most of us will encounter inner defense mechanisms and resistance or stubborn attachments that lead to confusion and cause us to lose direction and become stuck. A skillful guide can help us see those defense mechanisms for what they are and move beyond them. If we follow a humble way of accepting the need for guidance from masterful elders, we create communities of accountability and prevent the delusion of self-aggrandizement.

NORMA'S Reflections on Working with Her Clients

Many people have come to me for counseling after going on numerous altered-state journeys without a guide. Their minds are encumbered with Shadow material that has not been metabolized.

It is understandable that we cannot overcome our defensive patterns easily on our own. This is because our defense mechanisms were initially created to protect us. They worked hard to protect us from psychic harm, or the perceived possibility of it, for many years, and they won't simply disappear because we've adopted a new discipline or read more books.

Many steps on the path can be more driven by ego than you might realize. Your unconscious motives may move you toward change just to a certain point, but no further. Your lifelong protection strategies will perceive where you're headed as a threat and will work to undermine your conscious intentions to change.

Thus, I highly recommend that you find a teacher who can ally with you and help in steadily moving you toward integration and healing.

In this book, we have provided you with the beginning steps to help you recognize and confront your long-held defense patterns. The next stage of working with your Shadow patterns could be working with the full Journey to Completion system. You have already seen the map of the Journey to Completion, but each stage is intricate and far more involved than could be presented in this book alone.

If you feel ready to work with the Journey to Completion Wisdom School and Norma Burton, visit our website at *www.NormaBurton.com* for information on one-on-one sessions, retreats, and group work.

Enter the Liminal with Confidence

Now that you've explored the transformative potential of navigating the liminal realms and the landscapes of consciousness they reveal, you are prepared to engage with the Dreamtime with more skillful intention, preparation, and integration.

You've gained a greater ability to recognize and heal Shadow aspects, maintain lucidity during profound experiences, and embrace the inherent goodness and interconnectedness of all things.

So, embark on your personal journey toward wholeness and collective healing, equipped with the wisdom and tools to transform not only yourself into a more impeccable human but also the world around you into communities of solidarity and trustworthiness.

Notes and Illustration Credits

1. F. Vazza et al, "The Quantitative Comparison between the Neuronal Network and the Cosmic Web," *Frontiers in Physics* (2020).
2. Jan Dirk Blom, *A Dictionary of Hallucinations* (Springer, 2009).
3. T. W. Lumpkin, "Perceptual Diversity: Is Polyphasic Consciousness Necessary for Global Survival?," *Anthropology of Consciousness* (2001): 12: 37–70.
4. Stephanie Hegarty, *"The Myth of the Eight-Hour Sleep."BBC News*, 22 February 2012. https://www.bbc.com/news/magazine-16964783
5. David K. Randall, *"2. Light My Fire," Dreamland: Adventures in the Strange Science of Sleep* (W. Norton, 2012), 17–18.
6. Joseph Campbell, *The Hero with a Thousand Faces* (New World Library, 2008).
7. Victor Turner, *The Ritual Process: Structure and Anti-Structure* (Routledge, 2017).
8. L. Loewenberg, *Dream on It* (St. Martin's Griffin, 2011).
9. John F. Hughes, "Dreams, Myth, and Power." *Dreaming*, vol. 27, no. 2, 2017, 161–176.

Illustration Credits

Fig. 1: *Seek Safe Container.* Diagram by Norma Burton.

Fig. 2: *Outer/Inner Shadow.* Chart by Norma Burton.

Fig. 3: Magnússon, Finnur. *Yggdrasill, the Mundane Tree* (1859). Vintage Norse mythology. Print, color, 18 x 12 cm. Boston Public Library. CC BY-SA 3.0

Fig. 4: Rose, Vita. *Guadalupe de la Cruz Rios.* National Museum of the American Indian, Smithsonian Institution (NMAI-372_pht_001_P33763). 2007.

Fig. 5: Maurer, Markus. *Meme of Plato's "Allegory of the Cave"* (cropped), 2015. https://commons.wikimedia.org/wiki/File:Plato_Cave_Wikipedia.gif

Fig. 6: *The Journey to Completion Map*. Illustration by Norma Burton, 2020.

Fig. 7: *The Ascent into the Dreamtime*. AI illustration created by Nisha Burton, 2024.

Fig. 8: *Altaj-Kizi Samandob (Tungur) Rajolata – Drawing on an Old Shaman Drum*. Scanned by Szilas from the book *A honfoglalók műveltsége (Culture of the Early Hungarians)*, www.helikon.hu, 2018. https://commons.wikimedia.org/wiki/File:Image_on_a_shaman_drum.jpg

Fig. 9: *Altai Shaman Drum with the Skin of a Horse on a Rod*. Scanned by Szilas from the book *A honfoglalók műveltsége (Culture of the Early Hungarians)*, www.helikon.hu, 2018. https://picryl.com/media/altai-shaman-drum-with-the-skin-of-a-horse-on-a-rod-0b46a3

Fig. 10: *Sami drum, probably from Lule Lappmark*. Bowl drum. 40 x 27 cm. Described and depicted by *Johannes Schefferus* in his book *Lapponia* (1671); later described as No. 64 in Ernst Manker's *Die lappische Zaubertrommel* (1938). Schefferus says that it belonged to chancellor Magnus Gabriel de la Gardie; later in 1693 in Antikvitetskollegium. Statens Historiska Museum, Stockholm (SHM 360:2). Now at Nordiska museet. *https://commons.wikimedia.org/wiki/File:Sami_drum_from_lule_lappmark_top.jpg*

Fig. 11: *Nordic Sami Naero Runic Shaman Drum Mythology from Friis, 1871*. Project Runeberg.
Sami drum of undefined origin. Described and depicted by *Jens Andreas Friis* in his book *Lappisk mythologi, eventyr og folkesagn* (1871); later also discussed in *Sigurd Agrell*'s *Lapptrummor och runmagi* (1934). Now lost, according to in Ernst Manker's *Die lappische Zaubertrommel* (1938; p. 63). https://commons.wikimedia.org/wiki/File:Nordic_Sami_Naero_Runic_Shaman_Drum_Mythology_from_Friis_1871.jpg

Fig. 12: Anaroza. *A God's Eye, or Ojo de Dios, from Quemado Mountain, San Luis Potosi, Mexico*, 2007. https://commons.wikimedia.org/wiki/File:Ojo_de_dios_anaroza.jpg

Fig. 13: Mat, Juan Carlos Fonseca. *Cuadro de Estambre (Nierikas): Arte del Pueblo Wixárika (Huichol)*, 2019. https://commons.wikimedia.org/wiki/File:Cuadro_de_estambre_del_pueblo_wix%C3%A1rika_%28huichol%29_I.jpg

Bibliography

Books

Abelar, Taisha. *The Sorcerer's Crossing*. Penguin, 1993.

Aixalà, Marc. *Psychedelic Integration*. Synergetic Press, 2022.

Blake, William. *Songs of Innocence and of Experience*. S.L. Collectors Library, (1794) 2019.

Blom, Jan Dirk. *A Dictionary of Hallucinations*. Springer, 2009.

Buxton, Simon. *The Shamanic Way of the Bee: Ancient Wisdom and Healing Practices of the Bee Masters*. Destiny Books, 2006.

Campbell, Joseph, Phil Cousineau, and Stuart L. Brown. *The Hero's Journey: Joseph Campbell on his Life and Work* (The Collected Works of Joseph Campbell). New World Library, 2014.

Campbell, Joseph. *The Hero with a Thousand Faces*. New World Library, 2008.

Castaneda, Carlos. *The Art of Dreaming*. Element, 2004.

Donner, Florinda. *Shabono*. Harper Collins, 1992.

Donner-Grau, Florinda. *The Witch's Dream*. Penguin, 1997.

Eliade, Mircea. *Shamanism: Archaic Techniques of Ecstasy*. Princeton University Press, 2004.

Gendlin, Eugene T. *Focusing*. Bantam, 1982.

Herbert, Frank. *Dune*. Ace Books, 1965.

Kahn, Matt. *Whatever Arises, Love That: A Love Revolution That Begins with You*. Sounds True, 2016.

Karma-Gliṅ-Pa, Padma Sambhava, Gyurme Dorje, Graham Coleman, Thupten Jinpa, and Bstan-'dzin-Rgya-Mtsho, Dalai Lama XIV. *The Tibetan Book of the Dead (English title)/The Great Liberation by Hearing in the Intermediate States (Tibetan title)*. Viking, 2006.

Laberge, Stephen, Howard Rheingold, and Ballantine Books. *Exploring the World of Lucid Dreaming*. Ballantine Books, 2007.

Levine, Peter. *Waking the Tiger: Healing Trauma*. North Atlantic Books, 1997.

Loewenberg, Lauri Quinn. *Dream on It: Unlock Your Dreams, Change Your Life*. St. Martin's/Griffin, 2011.

Moore, Robert L. *Facing the Dragon*. Chiron Publications, 2018.

Muraresku, Brian. *The Immortality Key: The Secret History of the Religion with No Name*. St. Martin's Press, 2020.

Neihardt, John G. *Black Elk Speaks*. University Of Nebraska Press, 2014.

Prechtel, Martín. *Secrets of the Talking Jaguar: Memoirs from the Living Heart of a Mayan Village*. Jeremy P. Tarcher, 1999.

Randall, David K. *Adventures in the Strange Science of Sleep*. W. Norton, 2012.

Redmond, Layne. *When the Drummers Were Women: A Spiritual History of Rhythm*. The Rivers Press, 1997.

Spencer, Robert L. *The Craft of the Warrior*. Frog Books, 2005.

Tenzin Wangyal, and Mark Dahlby. *The Tibetan Yogas of Dream and Sleep: Practices for Awakening*. Shambhala, 2022.

Turner, Victor. *The Ritual Process: Structure and Anti-Structure*. Routledge, 2017.

Journals

Hughes, John F. "Dreams, Myth, and Power." *Dreaming*, vol. 27, no. 2, 2017, 161–176.

Lumpkin, T.W. "Perceptual Diversity: Is Polyphasic Consciousness Necessary for Global Survival?," *Anthropology of Consciousness*, 2001.

Vazza, F. et al. "The Quantitative Comparison between the Neuronal Network and the Cosmic Web," *Frontiers in Physics*, 2020.

Broadcast Media

Hegarty, Stephanie. *"The Myth of the Eight-Hour Sleep." BBC News*, 22 February 2012. https://www.bbc.com/news/magazine-16964783

Oracle Decks

Burton, Nisha, and Norma Burton. *Lucid Dreaming, Lucid Living: Your Oracle and Guide to Mastering the Dreamscape*. Red Wheel, 2023.

Index

affirmations, 71–73, 222–23
An Da Shealladh, 17
apophatic and cataphatic, 215
assemblage point, 18–19, 140–41
attaining lucidity, 171, 177
auditory driving, 87, 90–91
axis mundi, 52–54, 105

bardo(s), 31, 138, 153
betwixt and between, 229, 259

dream signs, 170–71, 173, 200
dream yoga, 11, 31, 98, 137–38, 186, 197–98, 258

entheogen(s), 57, 80, 207, 230, 238–39, 254
entheogenic, 52, 233

gnosis, 232, 257, 259
Guadalupe (de la Cruz Rios), 21, 56, 58, 60, 67–68, 220, 227–28, 246, 250
gymnosophism, 85

hemispheric synchronization, 89
hozho, 221
Huichol, 21, 52, 56, 66, 154, 215, 218–21, 225–27, 236, 259, 261, 264

I-Thou, 13, 32–35, 203, 257
individuation, 45–46, 255, 259

inner guidance, 57, 74–75, 180, 202, 231, 254, 257
inner shadow, 50–51, 75, 187, 233, 239–40
intent, 52, 55, 64–65, 72–74, 134, 177, 209, 224–26, 233–34, 259

Journey to Completion, 47, 50–51, 66, 239–40, 242, 253, 262
Journey to Completion Map, 70

liminal, 9, 30–32, 54, 138, 153, 224, 229, 249, 255, 257, 259, 262
lucid dream, 97–98, 107–8, 133–35, 185, 193, 208

maintaining lucidity, 177, 179–80, 182
middle world, 104–6, 108–9, 143
mnemonically induced lucid dreaming (MILD), 177
monophasic, 40–42

nagual(s), 18–21, 140, 183
nightmare rewrite technique, 189, 192–93
nightmare, 108, 184–85, 187–88

oneironaut, 30,
out-of-body experience (OBE), 108–9, 136
outer shadow, 50–51, 75, 187, 190, 233, 239–40

plant medicine(s), 13, 35, 52, 59, 80, 130, 216, 222–23, 237, 239, 259
polyphasic, 40, 42–44, 135, 178, 254
power animal(s), 12, 19, 75, 86, 119–21, 126, 128, 189, 208, 257
psilocybin, 9–11, 228, 238–39, 243–44, 246–48
psychonaut(s), 13, 30, 55, 63, 65, 103, 255
psychonavigation, 13–14, 27, 32, 47, 80–81, 133, 156, 165, 254–55, 258

REM cycles, 157, 159–60, 182
rite of passage, 154, 243, 246

second sight, 17–18, 44, 140
shadow (integration) work, 126, 180, 234–35, 259
shadow(s), 139, 176, 184–85, 187–88, 204, 223, 227, 236, 239, 254
shadowy, 57, 73, 111, 191, 204, 238
shape-shifting, 208
sleep paralysis, 90, 108–9, 188
state checks, 171–73, 179

The Call/The Calling, 36, 39, 60, 70–72, 73, 80, 139, 226
threshold guardians, 72, 74, 77–78, 80, 218, 222–23, 230, 234
threshold, 65, 73, 96, 116, 122, 141, 152, 223, 227
Tibetan Book of the Dead, 31, 197
trance, 34, 80, 85–91, 95–96, 180, 254
transmutation, 57, 76–77

underworld, 66, 71, 76, 104–106, 108, 110–15, 143, 154, 220, 223
upper world, 104–8, 113, 143, 180–81, 201

Via Negativa, 73–74, 111, 226
Via Positiva, 73–74, 111, 226

wake back to bed (WBTB) technique, 178
warrior move, 79
wisdom traditions, 11, 15–16, 52, 65, 119, 137, 219, 258

About the Authors

Photo by Nisha Burton

NORMA J. BURTON is a master of transpersonal psychology and scholar of world religions, specializing in Buddhist psychology, Jungian dream work, and trauma healing. With nine years of advanced academic degrees and more than 30 years of apprenticeship with Indigenous elders, Norma brings a rare level of expertise in guiding the exploration of the psyche, dreamtime, and altered states of consciousness. She has led thousands of people in the skill of integrating gifts of lucid exploration to become impeccable with power in daily life.

Norma has applied her skills in practical social change work by being a director of domestic violence prevention programs, an innovator in addiction recovery, and teaching leaders how to create ethical practices in the corporate work world. Her popular, somatic-oriented training process, Journey to Completion, is highly effective at addressing deep-seated issues such as healing from abuse, addiction recovery, improving communications within personal and work relationships, relieving anxiety, depression and phobias, and building self-esteem and personal empowerment. She is sought after by leaders in the corporate and non-profit sectors, university professors, psychologists, medical and religious professionals. A guest lecturer and workshop leader, Norma teaches in the USA and internationally.

For more information visit:
NormaBurton.com, *JourneytoCompletion.com*, and *LucidDreamingLucidLiving.com*

ABOUT THE AUTHORS

Photo by Nate Woods

NISHA BURTON is a skilled dream worker and psychonavigation expert, trained in the art of journeying into the deep subconscious from a young age. For the past decade, she has been immersed in the practice of lucid dreaming. In addition to her natural proclivities, she has studied the works of Stephen LaBerge, Tibetan Dream Yoga, and countless other lucid dreaming experts. She weaves the information that she has learned from masters into her own first-hand, advanced experience in the lucid dream realms. A professional filmmaker, digital artist, virtual reality expert, and branding strategist, she specializes in the craft of visual storytelling.

She is a sought-after speaker and teacher at universities and conferences because of her expertise in storytelling through various high-tech mediums. She is a Brand Strategy consultant for Fortune 100 companies.

For more information visit:
NishaBurton.com and
LucidDreamingLucidLiving.com

FINDHORN PRESS

Life-Changing Books

Learn more about us and our books at
www.findhornpress.com

For information on the Findhorn Foundation:
www.findhorn.org

Scan the QR code and save 25% at InnerTraditions.com. Browse over 2,000 titles on spirituality, the occult, ancient mysteries, new science, holistic health, and natural medicine.